Zen showed me the way

Man has no fate except past deeds;
No Hell but what he makes;
No Heaven too high for those to reach
whose passions sleep subdued.

From *The Light of Asia*

EDWIN ARNOLD

ZEN showed me the Way

. . . to peace, happiness and tranquility

by SESSUE HAYAKAWA

EDITED BY CROSWELL BOWEN

LONDON · GEORGE ALLEN AND UNWIN LTD

*This book has been printed in Great Britain by
offset litho at Taylor Garnett Evans & Co. Ltd,
Watford, Herts, and bound by them*

This book is dedicated to Thomas H. Ince, who first encouraged me to become an actor in motion pictures, and to Cecil B. De Mille, who was most generous not only with artistic instruction at the beginning of my career but who also gave me courage.

May the souls of these two benefactors live in peace and everlasting glorious guidance.

Acknowledgments

THE WORDS SET FORTH IN THIS BOOK ARE, FOR THE MOST part, the words of Sessue Hayakawa. They are a compilation both of what he spoke and put on paper over a period of the last two years in Japan and in the United States. In the spring of 1959, Mr. Hayakawa's autobiography, which was addressed to his fellow countrymen, was published in Japan. Early the following summer, the late Carlton Cole brought Mr. Hayakawa and me together in New York with a view to putting the distinguished Japanese actor's story into terms understandable to American and English readers.

Before making a decision, I decided to arrange to have the autobiography translated into English. I discussed my problem with Professor Ichiro Shirato, lecturer in Japanese at Columbia University, and he helped me commission Mrs. Makiko Doi, of the staff of Columbia's East Asiatic Library, and Miss Ayako Imai, a graduate student at Columbia, to translate the book. I am indebted to them not only for their work in the actual translating but for helping to convey the full implications of its meaning to Western minds. I am also indebted to the East Asiatic Library for books and information.

7

Studying the book and talking with Mr. Hayakawa made me realize that he did have a significant story to tell, but that we would need much additional information in order to make the book of interest to the West. I felt that Mr. Hayakawa's story would help bridge the East and West in much the same way Lafcadio Hearn did with his books.

Therefore, I decided to go ahead with the project and interviewed Mr. Hayakawa on a tape recorder for many sessions, spread over a period of several months. These interviews were then transcribed with great skill onto type-written pages by Mrs. Beth Freidel and Mrs. Florence Young, both of New York. This manuscript ran to several hundred thousand words. I am grateful to them, as I am to Mr. and Mrs. Robert Franklin of New York, for the transcript of tape-recorded interviews they held with Mr. Hayakawa for Columbia University's Oral History project. I am indebted to Mrs. Janet Scilipoti, of Chappaqua, New York, for typing parts of the manscript.

To Mr. Robert Young, who helped with research as well as with the cutting, arranging, and rewriting of some of the assembled 400,000 words, I am especially indebted. I am grateful to Miss Hortense Schorr, Mr. Harold Danzinger and Mr. Charles Powell of Columbia Pictures Corporation for photographs and information concerning Mr. Hayakawa's role in *The Bridge on the River Kwai*.

In the early stages of my talks with Mr. Hayakawa I learned that he had become a Zen priest. It soon became apparent to me that his stillness of spirit, his graceful manner with people, his charm, his sustained serenity, grew out of the teachings of Zen. It was not long before I became a Zen disciple. I am grateful for what he taught me about the Zen way. When the time came for us to talk about our book with the editor, Mr. Monroe Stearns, Mr. Hayakawa and I agreed that this autobiography would stress the part Zen had played in Sessue Hayakawa's eventful life.

I would like to feel that, in assisting in the preparation of this book, I have made it possible for others to share with Mr. Hayakawa in the peace, happiness and tranquility, that Zen has brought to countless numbers of persons down through the centuries.

CROSWELL BOWEN

Chappaqua, New York

Contents

Illustrations

Introduction to Zen

by Croswell Bowen

As our man-made, nightmare world becomes increasingly terrifying, only one course is left open to the sensitive, the civilized man. He must turn within himself to find the peace, the happiness, the tranquility for which he yearns and which he seldom achieves. Today man leads a life of desperation that lacks even the small solace, quietude.

When one begins to understand Zen and its implications, it becomes understandable why this ancient philosophy, religion, concept, attitude—call it what one will—has made such great headway, unaided by any commercial advantages, in the Western world.

In a culture motivated by pragmatism it is small wonder that Zen finds today an increasingly large following. It works. Furthermore, unlike so many of the religions of the West, it promises (and often provides) peace on *this* earth and rewards in *this* world.

Some years ago, a European college professor visiting in Japan was talking with some Japanese on the fifth floor of a hotel in Tokyo. Suddenly they all heard a low rumbling. "There was a gentle heaving under our feet," the European later noted. "The swaying and creaking and the crash of objects became more and more pronounced. Alarm and excitement mounted." The terror was all the greater because the great Japanese earthquake of 1923 was still fresh in memory. People rushed out of the room into the corridor to the stairs. Professor Eugene Herrigel, the European professor, asked the Japanese gentleman with whom he had been talking why he didn't hurry to run for safety. "I noticed to my astonishment," Professor Herrigel said, "that he was sitting there unmoved, hands folded, eyes nearly closed, as though none of it concerned him."

When after what seemed a lifetime the earthquake ended, Professor Herrigel's friend resumed his conversation where he had left off. "I was quite unable to pay attention and probably gave stupid answers," the professor later reported. "With the terror still chilling my limbs, I asked myself rather; What prevented me from running away? Why did I not follow an instinctive impulse? I found no satisfactory answer."

Later, he found the answer. The Japanese who had remained so unperturbed was a Zen Buddhist. He had put himself into a state of extreme concentration and thus become "unassailable."

Professor Herrigel stayed on in Japan determined to "penetrate Zen." He was advised that the best means of approaching Zen was through one of the arts, "because Zen has no theory and no dogma." He thereupon studied archery under a Zen master. Thus was born his book, *Zen in the Art of Archery*, which has become famous among the large following Zen has already acquired in the United States.

In this day of fear—fear of atomic blast, radiation poisoning, annihilating war—we greatly need the ability to become individually "unassailable." The frenetic pressures of modern life, the terrible materialism that permeates our culture, the widespread corruption, have left us little hope for a better life or a better world. Little wonder that increasingly large numbers of men and women in the West have turned to Zen to find peace of mind and stillness of spirit.

Obviously, in the few words allotted to this introduction, it is not possible fully to explain Zen which—it is often said—is not at all explainable in terms of our conscious mind or in any rational way. But there are many things about Zen that I feel can be explained through some assets that exist in our culture and especially in our American culture. We can take the first steps.

Much of Zen teaching, one soon discovers, is easily understood in terms of poetic concepts. Could Zen be a part of the universal language of poetry? As evidence, I submit two answers to a *koan* (a Zen question) which asked if there was a difference between the teachings of a certain Zen Patriarch and the teachings in the Buddhist Sutras. A Zen master answered, "When the cold weather comes, the fowl flies up in the trees while the wild duck goes into the water." A Zen disciple is asked to make of this what he will.

However, another Zen master, commented on the above answer as follows: "When water is scooped in the hands, the moon is reflected in them; when the flowers are handled, the scent soaks into the robe."

There is meaning here, but to try and pin down an explanation would be like tearing open a nightingale to find what produced the song.

Once a Zen monk asked a Zen master to tell him the secret of Zen. The master replied by asking a question: "What are your original features which you have even prior to your birth?"

You get it or you don't!

It is said that a Zen master clapped his hands together. Clap! He then moved his right hand and asked, "What is the sound of a single hand?" This *koan* has recently become so well known it has become one of Zen's clichés.

However, it is provocative—as it is meant to be. It helps one down "the great path [which] has no gates, thousands of roads enter it."

"When one passes through this gateless gate
He walks freely between heaven and earth."

One of the most beautiful of the Zen concepts, which recurs often in *koans* and Zen stories, is summed up in what is called the "soundless sound." Is the sound of one hand a "soundless sound"? A Zen nun spoke of listening to "the voice of the pines when no wind is stirring." Always in Zen there is the constant reaching for something forever elusive. One seeks Prajna, the truth that enables one to go on to Enlightenment, to Nirvana, to Satori. The way is called Tao.

Like "the soundless sound," there is "the endless moment." A Zen master explained that enlightenment was like sitting at a tiny window. A fleet-footed horse flies by close to the window. You have that tiny moment to gain enlightenment, that "endless moment." Professor Chang Chen-chi, an authority on Zen calls the Prajna, or truth, an "evasive shadow forever eluding one's grasp." One does

not fully understand but one can not resist something so
lovely as the words of Fu Ta Shih:

> Empty handed I go, but the spade is in my hands;
>   I walk on my feet, yet I am riding on the back of
>   a bull.
> When I pass over the bridge,
>   Lo, the bridge, but not the water flows!

Zen's origins go back five hundred years before Christ to
a man sitting cross-legged under a tree beside a river in the
northern part of India. The man came to be known as
Buddha, the Enlightened One. Despite its antiquity, Zen
Buddhism would seem to have arrived at certain truths
later to become identified with Christianity and other facts
which Sigmund Freud expounded in his theories about
the unconscious.

There is, for example, the story of the Japanese Empress
who vowed to wash personally one thousand beggars. The
one thousandth beggar was a leper. She hesitated but kept
her vow. Rays of light began emanating from the beggar
after she had finished her task. The beggar revealed himself as the Buddha.

Is not a Christian message conveyed by this story? Even
more direct connection between Zen and Christianity is
revealed by the experience of a university student who
visited the Zen master, Gasan. The student read aloud
passages from the Gospel of St. Matthew:

> "And why take ye thought for raiment? Consider the
> lilies of the field, how they grow; they toil not, neither do
> they spin: and yet I say unto you, That even Solomon in
> all his glory was not arrayed like one of these. . . . Take
> therefore no thought for the morrow: for the morrow shall
> take thought for the things of itself."

Gasan commented: "Whoever uttered those words I consider an enlightened man."

The student continued to read: "Ask, and it shall be given you. . . . For every one that asketh receiveth; and he that seeketh findeth; and to him that knocketh it shall be opened."

Gasan again commented, saying; "That is excellent. Whoever said that is not far from Buddhahood."

There is the Zen story of the little girl who became pregnant. She told her parents that the local Zen master had seduced her. The outraged parents went to the master and upbraided him. "Is that so?" was his only reply. He provided for the child and accepted full responsibility for its birth. Later the girl admitted that the father of her child was another man and that she had not known the Zen master. The parents went to him and apologized. Again he listened gravely and made the same comment: "Is that so?"

A Buddha nature or Christian charity?

Some of the Zen teachings have a real folk quality. There is, for example, the basic folk humor one finds in many cultures. There was a child protégé of a Zen master who used to meet another Zen master's protégé on the way to the market to buy vegetables. One morning the first child asked the second where he was going. The second answered, "I am going wherever my feet go." The first child told the master what the second had said to him. The master advised him to ask the same question again the next morning and then to say, "Suppose you have no feet, then where are you going?" When the first child again asked the second child where he was going, he said, "I am going where the wind blows."

The first child and his master were really confounded. Finally, the master suggested yet another try. "And suppose there is no wind?"

"Where are you going?" the first child asked the second child the third day.

"I am going," the second child replied, "to market to buy vegetables."

And that may be the origin of the shaggy dog story.

Drawing on the unconscious would seem to be part of the Zen way of life. Freud probed the enormous power of the unconscious, but Zen has always taken for granted that great art, great music, great poetry, stems from doing something without relational thought—impulsively. As Eugene O'Neill used to advise writers, "Just let your unconscious go to work." In archery it is a matter of shooting the arrow from the bow without consciously aiming. You point. It is perhaps not unlike the cowboys in the Old West who drew and fired almost with one gesture.

There is a rice paper on which Zen artists draw with ink. There can be no mistake. Once pen has touched paper, that is it. No paint to paint over. No erasing. Some of the most beautiful drawings in the world have been made in this fashion. This delving into the unconscious (if the Zen process can be described in Freudian terms) is related to another aspect of Zen—complete selflessness. It is as if you summoned a deeper strength, a universal force. You achieve what has been called "no mind." You are one with nature. Part of eternity. No longer the slave of time. This obliterating of the ego is necessary to achieve great art.

"This essential disinterestedness of the poetic art means that egoism is the *natural* enemy of poetic activity," wrote Jacques Maritain, the French philosopher. And Daisetz T. Suzuki, the great Zen authority and university professor, added: "When the egoism which is the natural enemy not only of the poetic activity but of every human activity worthy to be called truly human, is removed we have . . . super-personal energy or what I call the cosmic unconscious. It is by means of this that everything of creative art is accomplished. The satori-awakening is no other than creative intuition, which in terms of Buddhism is prajna-intuition." Professor Suzuki, who gave a series of lectures on Zen not long ago at Columbia University, adds that it is just this "creative intuition" that Zen discipline can attain for us.

One other clue to Zen is in the writings of Thoreau. In his *Walden* he wrote of being one with nature, and his philosophy is very close to the "serene reflection" of Zen. There is a rational explanation for the similarity between Thoreau and Zen. We know that Emerson had many books on Oriental religions in his library at Concord. Thoreau borrowed them and read them. Is American transcendentalism, then, in the tradition of the teachings of Zen?

There are a few practical instructions which can be set forth in learning how to practice Zen. Sessue Hayakawa stresses the importance of breathing in consciously and fully, and out slowly. He believes in stretching your body as if pushing out imaginary walls with your hands, your arms to the sides. With your feet, you also push an imaginary wall.

As for achieving "no mind"—the meditation in Zen—each person must probably develop the technique best suited to him. Professor Chang Chen-chi, a Chinese Buddhist scholar, has set forth suggestions for Zen practice.

1. Look inwardly at your state of mind before any thought arises.

2. When any thought does arise, cut it off and bring your mind back to the work.

3. Try to look at the mind all the time.

4. Try to look at this "looking-sensation" in daily activities.

5. Try to put your mind into a state as though you have just been shocked.

6. Meditate as frequently as possible. (Sessue Hayakawa also stresses this.)

7. In the midst of the most tumultuous activities, stop
and look at the mind for a moment.

8. Meditate for brief periods with the eyes wide-open.

9.′ Read Zen writings.

10. Practice Zen exercises with other Zen friends.

One of the easiest Zen exercises for a Westerner to
observe is the tea ceremony. Dr. Suzuki calls the tea ceremony, along with other artistic aspects of life, an expression
of the "spirit of eternal loneliness."

All one has to do in performing the tea ceremony is to
follow the ancient ritual. A few people gather in a small
room. Incense is burning. There is a single flower vase
which contains a single stem of flowers. There is a Sumiye
picture on the wall. In olden times, the warriors left their
swords outside. The guests listen in silence to the boiling
of the water for the tea. You sit cross-legged on the floor.
The tea utensils are beautiful but in quiet good taste. You
examine them carefully. There is some little talk about
the tea utensils or the beauty of the picture on the wall.
The mind is wonderfully lifted, Dr. Suzuki writes, above
the perplexities of life. "The warrior is saved from his
daily occupation of fighting. The businessman from his
ever-present idea of money-making. Here one may even
have a glimpse of eternity." You achieve a stillness of spirit.

Once a university professor came to inquire about Zen
from a Zen master named Nan-in. He poured the tea into
the professor's cup until it overflowed. The professor
pointed out that obviously no more tea could go into the
cup. The master then said, "You are, like this cup, full of
your own opinions and speculations. How can I show you
Zen unless you first empty your cup?"

It is perhaps difficult for all of us to empty the cup of
the mind, but the rewards of Zen are not inconsiderable.

As the Buddhist scholar, Nyogen Sensaki, "the homeless monk," has written: "If you have Zen in your life, you have no fear, no doubt, no unnecessary craving, no extreme motion. Neither illiberal attitudes nor egotistical actions trouble you.

"You serve humanity humbly, fulfilling your presence in this world with loving-kindness and observing your passing as a petal falling from a flower.

"Serene, you enjoy life in blissful tranquility. Such is the spirit of Zen."

Two Zen monks were arguing about a flag which hung in the sky at the top of a flagpole. One said, "The flag is moving." The other said, "The wind is moving."

A Zen master listened quietly and commented, "Not the wind, not the flag. Mind is moving."

The great Zen authority, Mumon, explains this dialogue further:

> "When the mouth opens
> All are wrong."

Zen showed me the way

1   The Hand of Destiny

NOBUNAGA, A GREAT WARRIOR OF ANCIENT JAPAN, ONCE marched out to meet the enemy with an army one-tenth the number of the opposition. To himself he said, "I will win. I am sure." But his men had doubt.

En route to the field of battle, Nobunaga paused to offer prayers at a wayside shrine. Then he told his men: "Destiny holds us in her hand." From his pocket he took a coin. "I will toss it. If heads comes, we will win; if tails, we will lose." He flung the coin skyward. It caught the sun and flashed and fell heads up. A roar of courage shook the small army. Eager to fight, Nobunaga's men won their battle easily.

"No one can change the hand of destiny," the victorious warrior's attendant told him after the fighting was over.

"Indeed one cannot," Nobunaga said, and held up the coin he had tossed. It had been doubled. Heads faced either way.

Your destiny and mine are charted in the heavens and written in ourselves. We think and we take action. Many times we take action without thinking. We work to achieve our designs, to go our ways as we wish. But the courses we follow in life as human beings of flesh and bones are not truly of our own choosing. All has been foreordained by the omnipresent force which motivates the whole of the universe. The man who is complete master of his destiny does not exist but in the deceiving fiction of ego. There is no such thing as coincidence. Nothing occurs without a sufficient cause. There is a cause for everything. Cause precedes; effect follows. Cause brings effect into being.

Our lives move inevitably along the endless track of eternity according to its inflexible decrees. Each of us is a part of all eternity, a grain of the infinite, indivisible from the stream which flows from a source no man has discovered.

The infinite is as a sphere which has no beginning and no end, and as they move, men mirror it. Life is a continuing cycle, and that which is the spark of life—the soul—is the essence of the mind. It is not born, so it can never die. It is not an existence. Thus it cannot perish. It is not the "I" of self. There is no such thing as "I." There is only oneness. We shape our ends only if what we pursue is in harmony with the great plan to which no key is given during life as we know it. All that we are is a result of what we have thought, and all that we become will result from what we think now, within the confines of what has been decided. It follows, then, that the event of today is but the echo of yesterday.

Each moment of being is a window on all eternity. Some men can see into this vastness, but most cannot. Ego and

the thirsts of desire keep them blind. What is to be, what
rests in the hands of destiny, is never revealed. Not that it
isn't there to see. It is. But it is obscured by man's pre-
occupation with the tangible world about him. The eyes
of men see, but in the very perception are clouded by
intellect, cloaked by the artificial wrappings devised by
humanity for, supposedly, its own solemnization.

There are times, however, few and infrequent, strange
and wonderful, when the destiny of a man makes itself
keenly felt. The sense of awareness of what is to be is given
to some men more than to others, and to still others never.
Looking back on the events of my life, my sojourn in
sangsara, the world of birth and death, I can count the
times when I knew I was hearing the voice of my destiny.
There have been moments when reality and unreality, the
past and the present, fused so that I knew I was close to
the cosmic mind.

All my life has been a journey. But my journey differs
from the journeys of most men, particularly those of the
West whose involvement is all too often with the here and
now and all which may be grasped and clutched and felt.
I do not journey toward what is generally conceded and
accepted to be the ultimate end of a man. For death is a
state of belief, and the acceptance of it a fallacy of mundane
preconception. Flesh and bones wither and die as does the
flower in earth from which water slowly evaporates. And
therefore it is held that a man dies.

But for some men there is no death. We walk in eternity,
from which we come and to which we return. No: my
journey is a journey to what we in Japan call nirvana,
which is a state of mind, an awareness of its undying
essence, in which one transcends relativity and becomes a
oneness with the universe—the Absolute Truth, all that
was and is and will be—and shares equally with everything,
living and nonliving, in the eternal. Therein one stands

immortal between heaven and earth. To this my way is the way of Zen.

For men such as I, who walk in eternity, who journey toward nirvana, there are many way stations along the path. Upon reaching them, we stop and rest. We become aware of being closer or farther away from our destination. Or we sense that we have come full cycle, and in a flash of realization a vista of eternity opens up. Light comes into the darkness. The future, the present, the past—all come together and fuse into the oneness of all. Cherish such moments should they come to you. Listen and learn from the inner voice which speaks to you at such a time.

To me, such a moment, at such a way station, came in Ceylon in 1957, when I was making the film, *The Bridge on the River Kwai,* one of the most notable motion picture successes of recent years. In it, my role is that of Colonel Saito, the stern commander of a Japanese prisoner-of-war camp deep in the jungle of Thailand, near the Burma border. Saito and his camp are there for one specific reason. He is duty-bound to see that a bridge is built across the Kwai for the railroad which will link the Bay of Bengal with Bangkok and Singapore and carry the Japanese Grand Army forward to forge still another link in the chain of victory it envisions as its destiny.

A professional soldier whom the vicissitudes of military life have made a martinet, Colonel Saito nevertheless is basically a decent man. He understands the reason of reason, but the demands of duty have deadened his understanding. Rooted in his devotion to duty are passions which are steadily consuming him. Vain, imbued with a false sense of superiority and importance, he looks upon himself as God, his camp as the world, his word as the law of it. He rules by force and fear, and is himself ruled by fear. His job is to see that the bridge is built, and, as it must be, built within a specified period of time.

For construction labor British prisoners of war, men captured when Singapore fell to the Japanese, are assigned to Saito's command by General Yamashita, in whose image the colonel sometimes sees himself, and whose barbaric example he follows. The prisoners are led by a quietly fanatic military disciplinarian, Colonel Nicholson, a heroic man, but at the same time a stupid, foolish one.

When the project of the bridge is assigned to him, Colonel Nicholson considers it a task to be performed and completed in the best British tradition. He organizes construction entirely. Painlessly, with unabashed confidence and cold, relentless logic, he usurps Colonel Saito's authority and responsibility and proceeds to make the building of the bridge over the River Kwai a distinctly British undertaking to which the presence of their captors seems only incidental to the purpose of himself and his men.

Until Colonel Nicholson evolves and presents his British plan for building the bridge, work on it under Japanese supervision has moved slowly. The incompetence of the Japanese engineer in charge and the feigned inability of the prisoners to work effectively have produced little progress. Time has begun to run out. With each day lost, Saito's apprehension grows. His duty is clear. He must have the bridge completed by a certain date. High military and government officials will be aboard the first train. They will expect everything to be perfect, will brook no excuses. If he fails, if the bridge is not finished, Saito knows he has no recourse but to commit hara-kiri.

It seems inevitable that self-destruction will be Saito's fate. Work on the bridge is nearly at a standstill. Saito has begun to sweat in fear of what failure will bring.

However, the plan put forth by Colonel Nicholson is one which will solve his problem. But it compromises his honor as a Japanese and a senior officer of the Japanese Grand Army. Yet he bends, and accepts the British solution. Nicholson's mastery of the situation, almost without

Saito realizing what happens, reduces, degrades and humiliates him. In a flash the hunter becomes the hunted.

Having capitulated, Saito knows the task entrusted to him will be performed. He is a beaten man. The British will succeed where he felt, in his heart of hearts, he would fail. It is as if the enemy has stripped him of his soul. Now loss of face, the grinding down of honor, refutation of what he believed to be his divine destiny—all this demands that he pay the last full measure. Alone in his quarters, he prepares to commit hara-kiri. He writes his last letter home, to Japan, to his wife and children.

As I sat before the camera in the character of Colonel Saito, at his desk in his quarters, the pictures of his loved ones before him, a vase of white blossoms nearby, the past and the present became one. The real and the unreal fused together. Time stood still; eternity yawned. The final strokes of black ink brushed upon white rice paper conjured a memory long buried deep in my unconscious. It broke the surface like a lotus bud and unfolded as if for the first time. What was the present in Ceylon became the past in another place, in another time, more than fifty years ago, when an eighteen-year-old youth knelt in a pool of soft light from white candles and composed a poem he prayed would explain why, minutes later, he would raise an ancient dagger against himself in protest against his destiny.

I was that youth. Failure had brought me to the brink of self-destruction.

In 1907, I was to follow a career in the navy. But an accident, the painful result of taking a dare which challenged my honor and my physical stamina, inflicted an injury that destroyed my perfect health and with it my eligibility. I was dismissed from service.

My boyhood dream was to become an admiral, commanding men and ships, and the thought of my making a success of my life in the Japanese Navy was the source of tremendous pride in me on the part of my father. My failure wounded him deeply. My father was a high government official in Japan, the governor of a province. He was a man greatly respected by all.

For a long time after I returned home from Tokyo and the sad news of my dismissal from the navy became widely known, my father could not bring himself to speak with people as once he did. In his depression, he kept to himself a great deal. He avoided meeting with people unless it was necessary. In shame he averted his eyes when friends and others known to him approached him on the streets of the village near his estate. He dreaded to think of explaining my failure. He dreaded having to experience the condescension of the society in which he moved as a leader and example.

At home his relationship with me was strained, awkward, fraught with unspoken grief. He found it hard to understand what had happened and why I had precipitated the failure which brought humiliation to both of us. We lost the closeness we enjoyed in former days and could not speak.

For me, the months following my accident and expulsion from the Naval Academy comprised a season in a hell of my own making. The effect of what had happened to me, the strangling of my long-nurtured, coveted ambition, tortured my mind. I brooded and little cared what befell me. Depressed and despondent, I decided to commit suicide by committing hara-kiri!

To commit hara-kiri, or *seppuku* as the ancestors from whom the custom was taken call it, is to commit punitive suicide in the tradition of samurai discipline. The samurai is the warrior or military class of Japan. In it the custom,

since forbidden by law, was to permit a transgressor condemned to pay for a sin with his life to perform hara-kiri,
instead of shaming him by execution.

Until 1868, the Western world knew very little about the
terrible ritual of hara-kiri. But in March of that year two
young Englishmen were, by invitation, included in a group
called to witness an instance of it.

The human tragedy they saw was a harrowing spectacle
of a man carefully and slowly disemboweling himself
unflinchingly, without outcry or show of pain, climaxed
by the wild, powerful swing and descent of a keen-edged
sword in the hands of his attendant, a close friend, lopping
off the head of the victim. The noise of the blow, awesome
and final, followed by a profound silence, was never forgotten by one of the two witnessing Occidentals. The
ritual was as vivid to him in memory when he recounted
what he saw a half-century later, as it was the night he
saw it.

The man who committed hara-kiri that night in 1868, a
handsome young army lieutenant, was a samurai who had
been condemned to death for making a mistake in judgment—abusing his command and precipitating a military
attack on a foreign settlement in the seaport of Kobe.
Being a samurai, he was given the privilege of committing
hara-kiri. The samurai established the ritual in Japan.

Sufficient reasons for hara-kiri by a samurai were any
breach of trust, failure to execute a difficult task or mission,
a clumsy mistake, even—many years ago, before the Western
world became even slightly acquainted with Japan—a look
of displeasure from one's lord. Suicide was committed by
disemboweling oneself because the Japanese, like the
ancient Greeks, believed that the soul of a man dwells in
his stomach, and to cut open the body there is to free the
soul and reveal its nature, good or bad, pure or polluted.

My reason for committing hara-kiri was my failure to

succeed in following my chosen ambition to become a naval officer. The disappointment and humiliation this brought to me and to my father left me no other way.

On my father's estate at this time were two fireproof buildings. Their entrances were guarded by thick-planked iron-bound doors. Their walls were three feet thick. The buildings were used for the protection of family valuables and other properties against robbers and from fire. I had my room in one of these buildings, away from the main house, where, with a sense of independence, I could freely follow my own desires and develop and pursue my interests in painting, writing and other studies. The room was my refuge.

Following my dismissal from the navy and my return home, I found temporary solace in painting. I applied myself to a life-size portrait of Admiral Heihachiro Togo, hero of the Russo-Japanese War. He was my idol and exemplar when I dreamed of having a naval career. I had wanted to follow in his footsteps, to be just like him. No boy dreamed more of such emulation than I. This man too, I thought, I had failed as I had failed myself and my father. The portrait I drew was homage. I saw myself in the features I sketched, in the uniform which emerged on my board during the long hours I passed alone in my room battling my thoughts.

On the evening I selected for self-destruction, I was calmer than I had been in months. Neither expression nor action betrayed my intent. I took the evening meal with my family, my eyes rarely rising from my food, my voice a whisper when I spoke. I spoke only when spoken to, and very few of the words passed at the table were addressed to me. When the meal was finished and my father settled himself to smoke and enjoy a cup of sake, I excused myself and went to walk in the garden before going to my room to prepare. Kame, my dog, rose from his place near the garden steps and met me when I walked out into the night. He trotted obediently at my heels as I wandered in the moonlit beauty of the garden and paused to gaze into the unreflecting motionless water of the fishpond on which great lotus blossoms rode like ships in a fleet.

The quiet beauty of the night did little for my troubled mind. More than six months had passed since the accident which led to my failure had occurred, but the sting of disappointment was as sharp as it had been in the beginning. My heart responded to nothing but painful memory.

I turned away from the pond and stooped to pat Kame. While I had stood peering into the darkness of the water, he had lain down beside me, his nose between his paws. I scratched his ears and, before I pulled my hand away, felt the rough caress of his tongue. "Why aren't you chasing rabbits?" I asked him. He barked and jumped about me as I made my way across the garden toward my room. "Go on," I ordered him when we reached the door. "Go back and lie down." I pointed, and he went back to his place near the main house.

My room was on the second floor. I went to it after locking and barricading the heavy outer door and made the room and myself ready for the ritual.

I spread white sheets upon the floor, stretching them to the four corners of the room. Against the broad, unbroken expanse of one wall I placed my portrait of Admiral Togo, flanking it with tall, white candles. Nearby I arranged vases of white flowers—acacia blossoms; and, in small burners, lighted incense. Its softly pungent aroma quickly filled the room.

Beside the spot where I would kneel and pray before the portrait of Admiral Togo I placed a small stand. On the stand I put a small plain wooden tray, and on the tray placed a dagger chosen from among the many samurai weapons passed down from generation to generation in my family.

According to custom, I concealed the dagger beneath a piece of rice paper.

All this done, I donned a pure white kimono and knelt to pray. I prayed to my father and mother and to Togo. I asked the forgiveness of each. Then I rose and went to my writing table and wrote farewell letters to my parents and to my brothers and sisters.

Finally, in the tradition of the ritual, I composed a long poem. It began: *Life is a dream, and though my body is a cherished thing, I must die and be reborn seven times to compensate for my failure and my deed of self-destruction.*

Then, before Togo, in the flickering light of the candles, I knelt to pray and beg forgiveness for the last time. And when I ended my prayers, I picked up the dagger. I wrapped its cover of rice paper about the handle and lifted the weapon respectfully to my forehead. Then I placed it in front of me. I stared at it. As I did so, I suddenly became aware of the enveloping silence. Only the faint sputtering of the candles disturbed the ghostly quiet of my room. In the silence, as I listened, the noise mounted to a roar.

Outside it was deep night—moonlit, flower-scented, soft, with a warm wind. It rippled the dark surface of the fish-pond and moaned through the bamboo grove at the far end of the garden.

With deliberation I slipped off the upper part of my kimono, making myself naked to the waist, and tucked the flowing sleeves of the garment beneath my knees so that, in death, I would not suffer the indignity of falling backward in a position of humiliation. This done, I grasped and raised the dagger with my right hand. With the index finger of my left I found the traditional point of penetration: one inch below the navel, four inches to the left of it. I did not hesitate. Drawing a breath, I quickly drove the point of the dagger into my flesh. My whole body shuddered. The sharp, hot pain of the puncture raced along my nerves like electricity. I shook violently, like a man cold beyond endurance. Lights, brilliant in color, danced before my eyes. A thunderous roaring crashed in my head.

Then it was as if a giant sledge hammer were hitting me in the back, pounding relentlessly. My head seemed to shoot toward the ceiling and strike it. My entire body was swimming in pain. I gritted my teeth and slowly drew the dagger to the right, but my hand became weak and powerless as the keen, fine-tempered blade began to slice across my belly. I faltered and withdrew the dagger, slipped into unconsciousness, then became lucid, then delirious.

Blind rage and the insane urge to succeed forced me to plunge the point of the dagger into my stomach again and again (thirty wounds were counted later) before I once more lapsed into unconsciousness and tumbled forward between the candles before the drawing of my idol Togo. Beyond the door of the building a dog was barking and howling in frenzy.

Then there was nothing.

2 A Fatal Dive

SESSUE IS NOT MY GIVEN NAME. IN MY FAMILY I WAS CALLED Kintaro; and by my boyhood friends, Kimbo. I did not assume the name of Sessue until I settled in Los Angeles and began my career as an actor.

I was born on June 10, 1890, in the main house of my father's estate in Nanaura township, a settlement of fishers and farmers on the southern coast of the Boso Peninsula— the thick stubby finger of Honshu, largest of the four main islands comprising Japan. The Boso Peninsula bounds Tokyo Bay on the east and divides it from the Pacific Ocean. Nanaura is in the prefecture, or province, of Chiba, which embraces the peninsula. Yoichiro Hayakawa, my father, was governor of Chiba Prefecture. I was his fifth and last child, his third son. My mother's name was

Kane. She had me rather late in her life. She had borne her first child, my elder brother Otojiro, twenty years before; my sister Tokiko sixteen years before I was born, my other brother Torao fourteen years before, and my sister Tokuko ten years before.

By birth I am a nobleman, and of the landed gentry. I am a samurai, a member of that caste of warrior knights which came into being in the twelfth century in Japan.

The samurai of old were a military clan. Until they increased in power and importance and came into their own, the samurai served as tax collectors and warriors of the powerful feudal families which, although an emperor existed, truly ruled the country. The greatest of these families was the Fujiwara, which controlled Japan for four hundred and fifty years, from A.D. 669 to 1120.

Fujiwara power and influence waned about the time the samurai began to grow in strength. Soon it was the warrior knights who held the upper hand. They fought among themselves for supremacy. The battles ended in victory for one of the first samurai clans, the Minamoto, or Genji, under whose patronage and protection my family—the Hayakawa—survived and flourished during the turbulent early years of Japanese civilization.

The Minamotos lost before they won, however. For after the decline of Fujiwara power, the samurai factions were many and chaos ensued until the middle of the twelfth century when another early clan, the Taira, waged war with the Minamoto over who should become the ruler. The Taira won, and dominated the royal court until it, too, went the way of the Fujiwara. Then the Minamotos rose and came to ruling power.

The roots of my family are deep in Japan. The Hayakawa line can be traced back more than 2,600 years to the antiquity before the birth of Christ, into the mists of time as we know it, where history is fragmentary—sometimes more legend than fact.

The thirteenth century witnessed the rise to power of Japan's first military dictatorship. It was headed by a Genji, Minamoto Yoritomo, a romantic and powerful figure, who made his capital at Kamakura, a fishing village near what is today the port of Yokohama. Before he came to power he maintained a castle-fortress near the ancestral seat of the Hayakawas, who allied themselves with him. And when Yoritomo went to Kamakura to establish himself as the leader of Japan, my forebears remained in charge at his castle. From Kamakura, the Minamotos reached out to down the last of the Tairas and make their grip firm.

It was Minamoto Yoritomo who led and raised the samurai to dominance. They became omniscient in political, social and economic affairs. They also became exceedingly class conscious.

The samurai worked hard at distinguishing themselves from other factions. And, point by point, they formulated a code of conduct which is still positive in Japan today. This code is called *Bushido*, the Way of the Warriors. It is often referred to as "the soul of Japan."

As taught by Minamoto Yoritomo, *Bushido* bid the samurai practice and mature the military arts in themselves, be not guilty of any base or rude conduct, be not cowardly or effeminate in behavior, be simple and frugal in living habits, keep promises, share a common fate by mutual bondage in defiance of death or life. Rules such as these governed me in my childhood. And fortitude, generosity, compassion and straightforwardness were some of the watchwords of my early training. I was taught to hold meanness in contempt, to be truthful and just, and to be diligent in all I undertook to do. One sees the basis of such guidance in these points of what is known as the samurai creed:

I have no divine power; I make honesty my power.
I have no magic power; I make inward strength my
    magic.
I am neither life nor death; I make the Eternal my life
    and death.
I have no body; I make fortitude my body.
I have no armor; I make good will and righteousness
    my armor.

I was schooled to have a strong sense of the right, and
both my parents emphasized I should never forget "You
are a samurai!" I remember my father telling me, not
long after I began to go to school: "The Hayakawa is a
family of honor, Kintaro. We are respected for our justice
and humanity. You must always hold our honor sacred.
Do what is asked of you, no matter how base the task may
appear to be. You are fortunate to live in comfort, free
from want, but you are not immune to the demand for
hard work."

This was one of a number of short lectures I received
from him in childhood. He had good reason to give them.
I was an active and strong-willed boy. Among my young
friends, I was always the leader—the captain.

To prove the truth of his words, my father assigned me
the job of cleaning the lamps in our house. Every morning
I had the responsibility of making the rounds of the rooms
to wipe the lamps free of soot and fill them with fresh oil.
There were about twenty lamps in all, and the work was
dirty and tiring. When I could, I hired the urchins of our
neighborhood to do the job for me, paying them for their
work—and silence about it—with spoonfuls of brown sugar
which was kept in a big earthenware jar in the kitchen.

My father also gave me the job of wiping dust from
the beams of the ceilings. I used to think he was terrible because he ordered me to do this as well as clean the
lamps. Since there were a number of servants in our

house, I naturally felt the jobs I had to do should be theirs.

However, my father said: "I let you clean the lamps because I do not want you to grow up a soft man of a rich family. I let you wipe ceilings because I think you might grow taller, and your chest become broader."

He was right. Money and material comfort should not be made excuses for bypassing the hard work concerned in living the good life. I have known rich men whose wealth has brought them nothing but suffering and pain.

As I remember, the servants took pride in seeing the youngest member of the family at work. They were very kind to me and helpful. Now and then, when I grew weary from stretching to brush the beams of the ceilings and blinked away tears of frustrated determination, a larger hand than mine would take the cloth and finish my work in silence.

Two of my father's servants were great favorites of mine. I made them my charges and took special care of both. They were handicapped and deserved a greater measure of understanding, indulgence and kindness. One, Torakichi, who was dumb, was a boy close to my own age. I called him Tora. The other, Hisataro, was a hunch-backed old man who suffered from asthma and waged a constant bone-wracking battle to breathe. His appearance and condition made him suspect, though he was harmless, and he was disliked by all but me.

I was told that my father was very pleased with me because of the sympathetic attitude I showed toward these two servants. He himself was very strict and conscious of his position as governor of Chiba Prefecture. Greatly responsible for my father's serious, no-nonsense nature was the fact that the heads of the Hayakawa family had been governors of Chiba for more than five generations. Thus, he ruled people with an authority born of long family tenure and tradition. My father was possessed of a strong, deeply engrained sense of duty, both paternal and professional.

But I could not bring myself to rule people as he did. Summary exercise of authority is alien to my nature. If I asked a favor or gave an order, I followed it with a reward of some sort. Perhaps, if destiny had not decided otherwise, and my actions had not bent me in other directions, I would be governor of Chiba today. I cannot recall if I ever desired to be. But if I did, I know that becoming governor would not have depended upon my will alone.

Nanaura township is on a coast swept by wind and waves. The rough climate of the region leaves its mark on the people, sturdy, hard-working fisherfolk. Those I knew learning was present. They thought I was not a person to in boyhood saw something in me that I was a long time stay in Nanaura, but in the future would go to Tokyo and become a famous man.

My father thought a great deal about making the belief of the people come true. When I was in the second or third grade, he called me to him one evening after dinner.

"Kintaro, I have been thinking about what you should be in later life," he said. "About your profession. I should like you to make your career in the navy."

"The navy, Father?"

"It is an honorable way. You will go to the Navy Preparatory School in Tokyo when you are finished with school here in Nanaura." He placed a hand on my shoulder and smiled down at me. "Now," he said, "go tell your mother your ambition."

I told my mother and Tora and Hisataro. It was not long before the people also learned that Kimbo was to be an officer in the emperor's navy. The choice of career was not mine, but I made it my own. In Nanaura, the people accepted the news as gospel. "Kintaro Hayakawa will make his life in the navy," they said. "He will rise high to become an admiral." To them, there were no two ways about it.

After I was graduated from grammar school in Nanaura, I was enrolled in the Navy Preparatory School. By that time, I was caught up in ambition to succeed. Success in the navy was my cherished objective. I was convinced the navy would be my life. Then, to heighten and intensify my devotion to my ambition, came the Russo-Japanese War. I was deep in my studies at the naval school when it began on February 6, 1904.

On February 9 there was a wild celebration at the school when the news arrived that our ships had sunk two large Russian cruisers, the *Variag* and the *Korietz*, off the coast of Korea, near Chemulpo. We students were all but set afire by the event.

As the months passed, we followed the progress of the war and debated the tactics of our admirals. The brilliancy of one, Admiral Heihachiro Togo, was a source of pride in us all. Togo was Togo the Invincible. And when he directed the Japanese fleet to complete and overwhelming victory over the Russian warships in the Battle of Tsushima Bay on May 27, 1905, the whole of Japan was swept by a wave of patriotic emotions.

Under Togo's command, the emperor's fleet destroyed that of the Rusian czar, commanded by Admiral Rojdestvensky, off the island of Tsushima in the narrow stretch of water between Korea and Japan. Japanese guns and torpedoes sank ship after ship: the battleships *Kniaz Suvaroff, Alexander III, Osliabya, Navarin, Sissoi Veliki* and *Borodino*; the cruisers *Dmitri Donski, Adm. Nakhimoff, Vladimir Monomach, Adm. Oushakoff, Zhemchug, Izumrud* and *Svietiana*. Russia suffered the loss of ten thousand men. Japanese casualties numbered less than one thousand.

With many others, I looked upon Togo as a god. He became my idol and example.

My studies at the naval school were hard, but far from dull. The war gave life to the subjects. Along with navigation and seamanship in general, I kept my body fit learning and practicing judo and *kendo*.

Kendo is the Japanese art of fencing. The perfection of ability in it involves exercises designed to keep the reflexes sharp, the body supple, the muscles in tone. It demands a high degree of alertness and absolute self-control. The weapons employed in *kendo* matches are harmless substitutes for the *katana*—the native sword of the samurai, so keen it can cleave a man from the collar bone to the center of the chest. The *katana* is often used in exercise, when a mistake in the swift movement of the blade can mean the cutting off of an ear or gashing oneself fatally. I first began to study *kendo* when I was six years old.

I was graduated from the Naval Preparatory School shortly before my eighteenth birthday, in June, 1908, and returned to my father's home in Nanaura to spend the summer. I had passed the physical and academic examinations and had been accepted by the Naval Academy in Etajima, where at last I was going to train to become an officer.

There was great happiness at home when I arrived. My sister Tokiko's daughter had become engaged and was preparing for her marriage. This, and my success at the naval school, excited everyone in my family. Especially my father. He saw a bright future for all of his children.

"When do you go to the Academy?" he asked me almost the moment I entered the door.

"In September. In September I will wear the uniform you have been waiting to see."

"Welcome home!" he said. "Welcome home, Kintaro—lieutenant!" He poured wine and we drank and were very close. He did not seem as stern as I had thought him to be when I was a child. He looked upon me as a man now, and treated me as one, though he did not reveal any relaxation of power. His word was still absolute in his house.

A few days before her wedding was to take place, my sister asked me to go with her to see a fortuneteller. He was an old man, a wisp of a being, hoary with age, and in the eyes of those who called upon his powers, the image of the seer they believed him to be.

"It is a good time," he told my sister. "All favors this marriage. Your daughter will be very happy."

Then he called to me:

"You," he said, "the brother. Come here. A great change will take place in your life very soon," he said when I stood before him. I smiled, amused. "I see you surrounded by water. But you will not become a navy man. You will change your profession. Instead, you will go to a foreign country beyond the mass of big water." He gestured in the direction of the ocean. "There you will become success- ful and become better known than a navy officer."

I was astounded! The old man knew nothing of my studies or my ambition. He could tell nothing from my dress. I was wearing a light summer kimono bound by a plain sash. They indicated nothing of my class or career. I was amazed at his accuracy—of his knowing I was training for the navy and his prediction that I would not become an officer.

"Well, Kintaro?" my sister asked.

"Well, what?"

"The prediction."

"A lot of nonsense," I said. I laughed, and after giving the fortuneteller a few yen, took Tokiko's hand and pulled her away. "Let's go home."

The first weeks of my summer vacation at home were

happy ones. In August, I went with five or six other boys—friends and former schoolmates in Nanaura—to the coast to swim and dive for abalone. One day we rented a small boat and rowed to where the professional abalone divers were going down as deep as thirteen fathoms—more than seventy-five feet—to bring up the black and silver-shelled seafood.

The professional divers went about their work wearing nothing more than loincloths and small goggles. Years of practice and experience in their craft had developed their lungs and breath control. Those we watched at work easily reached the bottom of the sea beneath our little boat.

"It looks easy, eh, Kintaro?" one of my friends said. We taunted one another about our diving prowess.

"How deep did you go?" I called to one of the divers when I saw his head break the surface of the water close by our boat.

"More than ten fathoms!" he yelled, and swam to put his abalone in the catch-boat with the rest he had brought up.

Ten fathoms! Perhaps more. More than sixty feet. My friends and I nudged each other and issued challenges.

"I will bet a dinner!" I said finally. "I bet a dinner for all that I shall touch the bottom!"

"Taken!" my friends cried. I scrambled to the bow of our boat and coiled the anchor rope so that it would run free. Then I slipped into the water and waited while my friends lowered the anchor of our boat into the water beside me. I took a firm grip on it and they let go. The heavy iron plummeted toward the floor of the ocean, pulling me quickly away from the pale green-blue surface waters into the darkness of the depths. I hung on for dear life, fighting the urge to breathe.

Just before I got to the bottom, I heard an explosion, a sudden roar in one ear. My head started to throb with a dull agonizing pain. I didn't know what had happened. Finally the anchor stopped moving downward. It and I had reached bottom. I opened my eyes and peered into the gloom while I groped for some token to show I had won my bet. The pain in my head kept me from focusing my sight. I felt around me until my hand brushed some seaweed and hit a rock. I grabbed them, let go of the anchor, and began to rise to the surface.

When I broke out into the air and sunlight my nose was bleeding and one half of my face was absolutely paralyzed. When I tried to yell to my friends I found I couldn't move my mouth without the pain in my ear searing like fire. I paddled to the boat, the rock and weeds clenched in one hand. I held them up while my friends pulled me on board. Then I let them go and sat holding my aching head in my hands, unable to speak. The clamor of my companions drew the attention of one of the professional divers. He swam over to learn what was wrong.

"Kintaro Hayakawa won his bet," one of my friends crowed. "He went to the bottom."

The diver looked at my bleeding nose and asked me if my head hurt. I nodded slowly and pointed to my ear.

"You've burst an eardrum," he said. "The terrific and sudden change of pressure punched a hole in it. Happened to me years ago." He grinned and removed plugs from his ears. "I burst both eardrums." He laughed and dived back to his work from the side of our boat.

My friends took me back to shore. My nose stopped bleeding, and after a time the pain in my ear went away. At the insistence of my friends, I went to see a doctor. He told me I had a tiny hole in my eardrum, prescribed some medication, and asked me to return and take treatment. But I didn't go back to him. I felt fine. The pain was gone, so I foolishly thought everything was all right. I went right on enjoying my vacation.

But the absence of pain and illness was only temporary. The pain returned and my ear became infected. And in September, when the time came for me to report to the

Naval Academy in Tokyo and begin my studies as a cadet, I was seriously ill. I saw the doctor again, but it was too late. My head swelled until I could not make my teeth meet. Three months passed before I was able to eat without pain and difficulty. I had no choice but to make my excuses to the authorities at the academy and remain in Nanaura to recover.

"What could have possessed you?" my father stormed at me when the worst of my illness had passed. "To risk your future to win a bet. You have a good brain, use it!"

The summer was over. Fall came and gave way to winter while I rested and recovered from my accident. In December word arrived from the Naval Academy that I need not return. I was expelled. My father read the letter and lapsed into damning silence.

In January, when I was well again, I went to Tokyo and applied for reinstatement as a cadet. I went through another physical examination, but it was of little use. I failed. And the decision on my expulsion from the academy remained final. The damage to my eardrum made me ineligible for naval service. I returned to Nanaura heart-broken and deeply ashamed. My dream of following in Admiral Togo's footsteps was shattered. I lost all sense of ambition. All goals seemed beyond my reach. Everything was at an end.

The greatest disappointment was my father's. My failure was a bitter blow to his honor and personal pride in me. It weighed heavily on his mind. My failure was his dishonor. He felt humiliated. We had little to say to one another during the months that followed my expulsion from the academy. I kept to myself, out of his way, and to my room. I worked on my portrait of Admiral Togo and fought with my conscience. Then the day came when I could fight no more.

3 Buddha's Lamp

IT WAS THE SOFT MURMUR OF VOICES, WOMEN SPEAKING OF
me in hushed tones, which woke me from the unconsciousness into which I plunged when my mind and body could
no longer bear the pain of hara-kiri. What was being said
was unintelligible; I heard only the music of it.

My first thought upon awakening was that I was in hell.
You have accomplished what you set out to do, I thought,
but the evil of it has begotten more evil. I believe in
heaven and in hell, and I seriously thought I was in the
void of eternal damnation.

As my mind cleared, the murmur I heard came into
focus. Snatches of conversation reached my ears.

"He is Governor Hayakawa's son . . . the youngest. . . .
Suicide . . . Hara-kiri . . . Poor boy . . . the wounds are . . ."

Slowly I came to my senses. The fog lifted from my

mind. I sensed movement near me and moved my eyes to see. Angels were standing by me. I was in a bed, and four angels were watching me. I can not be in hell, I thought, because there are angels. I must be in heaven. I have been forgiven. My sin has been purged.

But the angels were not angels, they were nurses. I was not in heaven, but in a hospital. I shifted my gaze among the faces bent to me. They were pretty faces, but the expressions were grave. No smiles.

After a time a new, masculine face appeared in the group ringing my bed. One of the doctors had come to check.

"He's awake, I see," he remarked, and to me said: "Can you hear me? You are all right. You are going to be all right." He smiled faintly and turned away after giving one of the nurses an order I could not hear.

"I'm alive." I said the words without sound, forming them with my lips only. I smiled and closed my eyes. But in an instance they were open again and staring at the ceiling. The enormity of what I had tried to do suddenly smashed at me. A surge of fear bathed me, and death seemed to hover very close. But I did not seek it now. Then another mood of happiness enveloped me. And another. The sensations of my emotions changed rapidly. Thoughts of life and death flashed in and out of my mind with the speed of light. Then I went to sleep.

I lay in the bed sleeping, feeling no pain, little sensation of any kind, when another murmur of voices awoke me a second time. I tried to speak and to move, but found I could not do either. A great weight was on my body; I was encased in a rigid plaster cast which held my body like a vise. Even when I took a breath there was barely room enough for my chest just slightly to expand.

I'm pinned down like some animal, I thought. Then I thought of hara-kiri and figured they had restrained me from harming myself further.

I know now that I little realized the seriousness of my condition. For the next day I asked to read a newspaper, and lay in bed idly turning its pages, reading the news as if on vacation. At that time it was not known whether I would live or die. In my delirium before the portrait of Togo in my room I had stabbed and slashed at myself many times; and, until I was found by my family, I had bled profusely, losing nearly three quarts of blood.

The doctors tried everything when I was brought in, beginning with a transfusion. I was a borderline case for days. Even after five weeks, one of my deepest wounds would not take treatment. In addition to ripping my flesh, the dagger had pierced and torn my intestines. The doctors sewed them back together and, until they knit and resumed their natural function, kept them drained of pus and lubricated through a series of rubber tubes which carried away the refuse of healing and fed in the correct amount of moisture—one drop of water per second at constant temperature.

After I had been in the hospital for about a month, I was told how I was found in my room at home. My pet dog Kame had walked with me in the garden that night. I shut him out when I went to my room. He lay down to wait for me, but as the hours passed, became upset and restless— disturbed through the strange sense of danger animals instinctively possess. He began whining and howling. He ran back and forth between the main house and the building containing my room until he attracted the attention of some of the servants. Kame had never been known to act that way before, so they followed him. And when he jumped again and again at the door of the storage building, they tried to open it and enter. Unable to do this, they called my father, who ordered the door broken in. To do so, six of the strongest men on the estate had to use a battering ram, axes and iron pry bars. After the door was smashed open they rushed up to my room and found me doubled over in a wide pool of blood. But it was Kame who saved my life. An ordinary mongrel dog. I have not been without a dog since then.

The long weeks I spent in the hospital gave me the pause I needed in which to think and reflect. The damage to my eardrum which had abruptly ended my naval career, shaming me in my father's eyes and him in the eyes of those he governed, had driven me to the edge of destruction. The dagger with which I had sought to protest the course of my destiny—what I had done with it—had now placed me on an unknown path. I had no thought of my future, no plans. The only thing I was certain of was my shame. Shame is a painful sensation. *Renchi-shin,* the sense of shame is called in Japanese. Sense of shame has an intense effect on a samurai. It illuminates the knowledge of guilt and is humiliating. A person reared by the *Bushido* code, such as I was, is required to know what will bring shame and to avoid it. I had broken the code when I foolishly neglected to have the injury to my ear treated properly.

When I had at last recovered and was released from the hospital, there seemed no place for me to go but back home to my father's house, to the very scene of my latest inglorious action. I could not do so. I was welcome there; I was expected to return. While I was still in the hospital my parents had exacted a promise from me to never attempt hara-kiri again, so that avenue was forever closed. Had I not promised I would have again taken up the dagger against myself. I was honor-bound to do so. But the promise now forbade it.

To go home to continued shame and disgrace was the last thing I desired. I could not bear the thought of seeing my parents or my brothers and sisters; of confronting my friends and the people of Nanaura.

On the day I was released from the hospital, as I was going down the front stairs, one of the doctors stopped me and asked: "What do you plan to do now? Not another rash . . ."

"No," I said. "That is forbidden now. I have promised."

"Then you are going home, Kintaro Hayakawa?"

I shook my head. "Not until I find and know why—the answer to it all. I cannot go home until then."

"You've been extremely fortunate," he said. "I should give thanks at the shrine if I were you "

"Perhaps."

I left him and walked down the road away from the hospital and in the opposite direction from my father's house. I couldn't go back. Thus, separating myself from my father, denying myself the strength of his love and understanding, I turned my thoughts to the search for solace that every man may make alone and in his own way. From the hospital I went to the foot of a mountain about half a mile from my father's estate. There, midway between the waters of outer Tokyo Bay and the heart of Boso Peninsula, was a Zen Buddhist temple kept by a priest with whom I had a slight acquaintance. I felt I could turn to him in my need.

The priest's name was Eichi. When I arrived at the temple, I found him sitting in the garden. I greeted him and stood silent and waited.

"You are Kintaro Hayakawa, the son of the governor," he said. "I am honored. Why have you come?"

"I want to become a priest."

"Why?"

"I must have purpose to my life."

"There is none to it now?"

"None," I said. "There was, but it is gone."

"What troubles you so deeply?" Eichi asked. He stared penetratingly into my eyes as if he was probing my mind, unrolling it before him like a scroll and reading it thought by thougnt. "Your eyes are dark mirrors."

"I tried to kill myself!"

He nodded as if I had made a remark of no more portent than point out the sun was setting. "Why?" he asked.

Somewhere, deep inside me, a valve opened. The words of my story roared forth in a torrent. "I am now eighteen— a man, but not among men. When I was small, a schoolboy playing at games of war, my father named my goal in life. I was to become an officer in the navy. I thought this was my destiny. To be an officer was my cherished ambition. My father's dream for me was my dream. I was to honor my family. But, instead, I have brought it nothing but disgrace. Just before I was to enter the Naval Academy in Tokyo I went for a holiday on the coast and injured my ear diving for abalone. The injury ended my naval career. I was expelled from service."

"Now you want to turn your face from the world you know."

"I tried to commit suicide and failed. The scars are still fresh. Here." I pointed to my stomach. "Why did I try? What was the cause? I cannot go home until I find some purpose. I must find some explanation, some consolation for the unhappy turn my life has taken. Everything has perished. What is there in the future for me? I want to become a priest. I must! I must see for myself the truth of the world!"

"You seem determined," Eichi said. He turned from me and fixed his gaze upon the image of the Buddha sitting just beyond where I stood. "Young man," he said suddenly, "why should you seek to take your life? That's the question. Do you know? It seems you don't. You despaired without knowing the cause. Life is precious. To take it by your own hand is to fly in the face of Buddha, hate when you should love. It is a crime for you to attempt such a thing.

Your attempt was perhaps the effect of the cause, but in your rashness you create the cause for the next life—when you will be a creature—by destroying the precious body given you by your loving parents. Why do you attempt self-destruction? Why would you give your parents such suffering, tears of tragedy? Your brothers and sisters and friends. Would you have them share your failure with heartache and grief? You are foolish! You only tried to escape from your skin—to save your skin—but not once did you think of anyone else. You are selfish! Of course, in that moment, you thought of nothing but the subject in mind—yourself. You were not concerned with others. What way is that to live?"

I protested. I told him about the effect of my failure on my father, the disgrace I felt and the humiliation I had forced my father to endure.

"Which is the greater disgrace now?" Eichi asked.

I had not thought of what I had done in this light. To fail to achieve my ambition was one thing. But to attempt hara-kiri . . . My father did not hold with this ancient samurai ritual. I stood puzzled by the question.

Eichi got up from the cross-legged position he had been sitting while we talked and took me by the right arm. "It is near time to eat," he said, walking me toward the temple. "Tell me," he asked as we stopped and stood for a moment beneath the overhang of the temple's steep sloping roof, "why haven't you tried to complete what you started?"

"I have given my promise to my parents never to try again."

"It is well," he said. The tone of his voice was warm and encouraging. "Come and eat. We will talk some more later."

"There is an old Japanese proverb which says, 'Destroy all passions when you light Buddha's lamp,' " Eichi remarked at the close of our meal, when we were again discussing my desire to become a Zen priest. "The way of Zen is not an easy way. It is not for the man who is lashed by the conscious passions of anger, hate, fear, doubt, remorse or envy. There is no room for the ego. There is no 'I'," he said.

"It is far easier said than done," I remarked.

"But you would learn?"

"I have given my promise. I must go on living, but not like this, hollow and without hope."

Eichi closed his eyes in thought for a few moments. Then, rising, he walked back toward the garden of the temple. He beckoned for me to follow.

When we were again in the garden, he directed I follow the curve of his arm with my gaze. He pointed up the slope of the mountain rising majestically behind the temple. It was twilight. About us was a stillness disturbed only by the faint whisper of early evening wind blowing from the Nanaura coast. High above us night mists had begun to close in about the mountain. "There is an old temple up there," Eichi said. "It is not used any more." He let his arm drop to his side and turned to face me. "If it is your wish to have peace and purpose, you must seek within yourself. Go there, to the temple, where you will be alone and be able to think. Perhaps, in time, you will see a pattern of life in the pieces you presently feel are all that there is. Take what you need and go. I will visit you from time to time. Yes, I will help you. Perhaps the way of Zen is the way for you. We will see."

I slept in the temple that night, on a thin mat in a small room set aside for the use of infrequent guests. I slept fitfully, my forehead and palms moist with mixed joy and fear. Eighteen is far from the age of wisdom. What I was undertaking was a mystery to me in every way. And it was to remain a mystery for quite some time to come.

The following morning I got ready to go up on the mountain. Eichi provided me with the first of the provisions I needed—rice, a bit of salt, charcoal, a mat to sleep on, seeds from which I later raised tomatoes, a few shoots from which I grew potatoes and corn. And books. He gave me six books from which I was to gain a beginning in Zen.

"I will see to telling your family," he said when I was ready to leave. "I will explain. Perhaps someone will visit you; perhaps no one. Read where I have marked in the books. Let what you read sink into you. Then search within yourself. Go now. The path to the temple is there." He pointed the way.

I left him standing in the garden of his temple and followed the path. The sun rose as I made my way upward. We climbed together. I found the morning mountain air invigorating; and though I tired as I climbed, my spirits quickened, the burden upon my mind seemed to grow lighter.

Upon arriving at the old temple, I chose a place to sleep, and stored what I had brought. Then I looked about. The temple was dilapidated as Eichi had said it would be; the grass roof was broken through, the doors and windows in sad repair. But, inside, the altar was intact, and upon it rested a statue of Buddha.

From the garden of the temple I could look down to the valley and beyond to the waters of outer Tokyo Bay. Now and then a ship passed, and it seemed as if I had only to stretch out my hand to touch it.

For the remainder of the day I investigated the temple and the surrounding area. I found a stream of cold, pure water. It ran freely down the mountain from above the temple, past it, and beyond toward the valley below. Late in the afternoon I bathed and sat, naked, drying in the sun, alone as I had never been alone before.

The first days and nights on the mountain were hard. When you have the time to think and reflect, your thoughts seem to multiply into an endless phantasmagoria. Memories are stirred like dust by a broom, and settle slowly, each shining by itself, as motes do in a shaft of sunlight. Fear and doubt assailed me. The frustration of ignorance confused my mind. All the passions Eichi said must be cast off gripped me by turns.

But gradually the atmosphere had its desired effect. The light of nature is impossible to cloak with one's own private darkness. The beauty of blue sky laced with white clouds, vivid green trees gently ruffled by warm wind, the special silence marking nature at peace: these things nullify man's resistance to life. One cannot stay angry forever. I could not.

"You must master yourself," Eichi told me when we first talked. "The passions must be subdued. Moral discipline is a prerequisite to the practice of Zen."

"I am a samurai," I said. "The *Bushido* . . ."

"Is only part of the way," he interrupted. "Remember this: Zen is not the way of the warrior, although Zen is the religion of the samurai. Therefore, it follows that Zen, not *Bushido*, was first. The strength of the samurai lies in an attitude of mind which puts the consciousness of self second to the task at hand. And what is the source of such an attitude of mind? Zen."

"What is Zen?"

Eichi smiled an indulgent smile. He waved my question aside. "In Zen, though morality is important, self-discipline is the stronger essential. Until you have mastered yourself, made your mind your friend, you cannot begin to follow the way of Zen. And policing oneself is a difficult task, as you well know. You have scars which prove your inability.

"You are a layman, Kintaro Hayakawa. The way is always harder for a layman. The Zen monk, such as I once

was, before becoming a priest, works from the outside to
the inside. The layman, such as you are, must break
through from the inside."

"What is Zen?" I persisted. "Where do I travel by working from the inside, from within myself?"

"It is easier to tell you what Zen is not," Eichi replied.
"But the aim of Zen is to enable you to understand, realize,
and perfect your own mind. Mind is the keystone. Mind!"

My first week at the old temple passed slowly, painfully.
Diligently I prayed to Buddha, daily prostrating myself
before the weathered, serene-featured image on the altar.
No inkling of the intense peace in those features reached
me. My mind continued to be a caldron of distracting
memories, happy, sad and terrorizing.

Routine governed the whole of my stay on the mountain.
Mornings, I was up before the sun. I washed in the stream,
and beneath a sky radiant with stars, only one edge faded
by the vanguard of dawn, I meditated, sitting cross-legged
like a yogi. In meditation I tried to subdue my anxiety,
replace nervousness with calm, order my thoughts, then
dissolve them. I meditated—tried to forget the self identified with my physical person.

You begin meditation by concentrating on one object.
As long as the object remains while you concentrate, your
consciousness prevails and you are unable to dissociate self
from yourself. Something gnaws at your mind—the why of
suffering, why you are born, why you must die, why you
must love something, why you are hated by something.

After ending my meditation I read for perhaps an hour
in the books Eichi had given me. Again and again the
books told me stories of the experiences of the great masters
in Zen. What events shaped their lives; what led to their
experiences of *satori*, the Japanese term for enlightenment,
or awakening.

Satori is the criterion of Zen—a spiritual experience so definite one is never mistaken in experiencing it. It is the sudden realization of the truth of Zen. It cannot be explained by the intellect. It cannot be brought about by intellectualizing. Logic has no place.

My hour of reading was followed by breakfast, cooked over a charcoal fire. While the food cooked, I did a little exercising—deep breathing.

"Tame the breath and you tame the mind," Eichi had admonished when we talked the night before I sought refuge at the deserted temple. The control of the breath is called *prayama*.

Then I ate. After breakfast I took a thirty minute walk before resuming my reading and meditation.

While in meditation, an inkling of why I suffered came to me. Tracing cause and effect made me see my suffering as a consequence, an effect. If it is an effect, I thought, there must be a cause. Nothing happens without a cause. I told myself, "To escape from your suffering you must hereafter cut off any cause that may bring suffering to you."

How simple to say, but how difficult to do.

Given that my suffering—the torment that led to my attempted suicide and the bankrupting of spirit which followed—was an effect, what was the cause? Revelation of this escaped me for a long time. Only after considerable meditation and study was I able gradually to reach the conclusions I sought. The knowledge came slowly. It seeped, forced from within as I developed my mental power and stripped away the layers of conditioning which bottled it deep in my subconscious.

The books I had also told me something of Zen origins. Zen is a form of Buddhism peculiar to the Japanese. Indian Buddhism, from which Zen derives, had its birth in the mind of Siddhartha Gautama (the Buddha, the

Enlightened One), a prince of India, born to grandeur and riches about the year 563 B.C.

Siddhartha Gautama lived a cloistered life on orders from his father until he himself was married and a father. Until then, he knew nothing of the states which characterize earthly life: old age and decrepitude, disease and death. That such results were the outcome of human life, the end of all begun by birth, shocked him into the depths of despondency and morbid reflections, and made his past and present happiness meaningless. "Gradually," according to one account, "the attraction of a different mode of life began to assert itself: a life not of attachment to things and people but of detachment and contemplation, in which the true meaning of existence might become clear."

The assertion of this attraction led Gautama abruptly to repudiate his wealth and material comfort to search for the deeper truth which came to be called nirvana.

Gautama's search for wisdom and sanctity took ten years during which he tried many directions, none of which led to his desire until the day he ceased to search. That day he sat himself beneath a fig tree which had broken through the ground the exact day he himself had been born. He sat as if rooted to the earth and vowed not to rise from the posture he had assumed until his aim was accomplished. All the emotions and passions of human existence assailed his mind. His will wavered and bent, but he resisted with his concentration. Thus, enlightenment came to him as he sat beneath the fig tree. In a single flash he had a vision of all eternity. Nirvana was his, and he was summoned. But he refused emancipation. Instead, he chose to remain of the world of birth and death and battle the characteristic of human existence which had motivated his search for the true meaning of life.

Siddhartha Gautama gained his insight into the mysteries

of life in the fifth century B.C. A thousand years later, the essence of what he taught was carried to China by a Buddhist patriarch named Bodhidharma. Japan, greatly receptive to Chinese influence until comparatively recent times, fell under the spell of the Zen philosophy sometime during the twelfth century A.D. Zen took deep root in Japan. It inspired, as it continues to inspire, some of the most beautiful sculpture, painting, and literature to come out of the East.

And, as Eichi told me, Zen, taken as the religion of the samurai, evolved the stern tenets of the way of the warrior— *Bushido.*

Zen Buddhists hold that the way of Zen is the nucleus of Buddhism, the inner core. Zen is the religion of life, essentially the acquisition of a new point of view on life which accepts the unity of all living things. For Buddha did not strive to learn the why of human existence. He pursued and found a way to live, and passed on a doctrine of how to live that releases man from the fetters his own resistance to life fashions.

To follow the way of Zen is to see into the nature of your own being, your self. And to achieve realization of self. But it is a self that is not distinguished by "I" and "Me."

"There is no 'I,' " Eichi impressed upon me. "There is only the fusion of self into life until they are as one."

Meditation played a large part in my fight to master my mind. But even before I could meditate productively I had to induce a level of concentration which would preclude all distraction. At Eichi's direction, I practiced *prayama*, sitting in the yogi posture and focusing on a cadenced count of each inhalation and exhalation— separately—one . . . two . . . three . . . through to ten, without interruption. Success at this tames the breath, making it subtle and light. But success is never immediately forthcoming. Any distraction necessitates starting the count over. And time and time again I was distracted by the sounds about me. The birds, chirping and fluttering their wings. The scurry of a rat through the tangled grass and weeds ringing the temple like a turbulent sea. Each time I had to begin anew. Finally, constant practice broke the barrier, and through this device I was able to enhance meditation.

Satori is not experienced spontaneously, although it seems to illuminate in that fashion. It is only one of the two vital factors which have sustained Zen spirit down through the years. Following the way of Zen also depends upon the *koans*, a form of Zen story, situation or problem.

Literally, *koan* means a public document, but no *koan* in Zen can ever be confused with a proclamation of government or the records of a trial.

It is by the *koans* that the teachings of the Zen masters are handed down and the disciple of Zen is led toward *satori* and the existence of doubt is tested. *Koans* are the harbingers of Zen understanding, yet they defy intellectual solution. In my books, I read:

"What is the sound of one hand?"

"When you have scaled the cliff and reached the summit, where will one more step upward take you?"

"When the Many are reduced to One, to what is the One to be reduced?"

Riddles? Nonsense? *Koans* are calculated to rip down the walls of logic. Meditation upon a *koan* concentrates the mind and stimulates the will to the highest degree. *Koans* seem meaningless, but behind their puzzles something is always implied.

"Are you the slave or the master?" Eichi asked. A fortnight had passed since I had climbed to close myself away. As promised, he had arrived to give me instruction.

"Your family prays for you," he said. "Particularly your mother."

"And my father?"

"He understands, I think. But he is one of the world of action, too much concerned with everyday affairs. He is a proud man, Kintaro. Your struggle means something to him, I'm sure, but his ignorance of its true nature is as much as yours. I don't believe you want him to accept the way of things blindly any more than you want to do so. His wounds must heal too."

I nodded.

Eichi picked up the book I had held when he arrived and idly turned its pages. "What have you learned?" he asked.

"So far, nothing."

"Then, perhaps, you have unlearned. There is no room in Zen for preconceptions. You must cast out everything."

"Then my mind would be a blank!"

He smiled. "You have learned something after all!" He closed the book and handed it to me. "I know that you find it all very hard. The meditation and the reading. You are eager to achieve some result, to discover some answer that will put a worth back into your life. You must have patience, Kintaro, patience. Have you read in this book and the others?"

"A little each morning. Before breakfast."

"Then you have encountered the *koan*. I want you to meditate upon this one: 'Who are you? What did your original face look like before your parents conceived you, before they themselves were conceived?' "

"There is an answer?"

"Why doubt it?" Eichi said. "Doubt is a poison you must expel."

"And you could tell me the answer?" I added.

"And if I did, what purpose would it serve? What someone tells you is not your own knowledge."

"But most of life, what a person knows, is learned!" I protested. "From others, teachers . . ."

"Most of the life you associate with this person." Eichi gently tapped my arm with the staff he carried. "In Zen you seek to transcend this life of birth and death. I can no more tell you the answer to that *koan*, than I can tell you the answer to the problem that first brought you to me. You must seek it yourself, in yourself. You know that. I must go now. Goodbye."

He left me standing before the decaying temple, and I stood there watching him disappear into the trees beyond the fallen wall that surrounded the old temple yard.

I saw only one other human being during the time that passed until Eichi returned to visit me. A woodcutter chanced by one morning shortly after sunrise, and called me when I was cooking breakfast. His voice was cheerful in its greeting, but I ran from him like a startled deer. I could not bring myself to say so much as one word. I fled into the forest beyond the temple and remained there until the man was gone. When I returned I saw that he had troubled himself to bank my fire after removing the small pot of rice I had been cooking. This small kindness shamed me. Still I could not have talked with him. I saw him again, two or three times more, before I left the temple and returned to the valley, but we never spoke. My sudden departure when he approached finally convinced him to leave me alone.

The most difficult task for any man is for him to find himself. The odds against his doing so are considerable. And what makes his search all the more heartbreaking is the fact that the barriers he comes up against as he searches are all of his own making.

Buddha's doctrine holds that man suffers because of desire—the urge to possess and keep all that is actually impermanent. Man insists upon making a supremacy of his person. He retreats into it and sets himself apart and resists life, all the while assuming egotistically that he lives life.

Finding myself was the task with which I was faced. And it was the task toward which Eichi's *koan* led me.

It was the beginning of fall when I went to stay alone at the temple. The foliage was still rich in color. The birds and squirrels and other small mountain animals were still about. Winter only showed itself at night, in the wind which kept me close by my charcoal fire until the last bit was consumed and it was time to sleep. But as the weeks passed I saw the seasons change. The green of the trees and shrubs faded to brown and red, the leaves withered and fell, pine needles dried and dropped like rain when the wind blew. The water of the stream became colder as the first snow gathered on the top of the mountain.

Before winter closed in, however, I was in good health. All my wounds were completely healed. The scars were tough. My body was well again. Now each morning before the sun reached its peak I practiced the movements of *kendo*—ritualistic Japanese fencing—until sweat beaded and rolled from my body. I fashioned a practice sword out of stout wood, and with it cut and slashed at the trunk of a dead tree, concentrating on synchronizing my mind and body in an alertness of reflex which is the key to *kendo*. Here again it was mastery of the mind. *Kendo* is an art strongly influenced by Zen. Dominion over the mind is paramount. The mind, which will stop continuity to apply intellect, must be forced into non-interference. In a contest the swordsman has no time to intellectualize. All action must be intuitive, positive, immediate and without interruption. Conditioned reflex is impossible. The course of action constantly changes. One must change with it.

My days on the mountain became weeks; the weeks, months. I saw no one but the woodcutter and Eichi until

one day, some two months after I went up on the mountain,
I had a visit from my mother. She came to bring me food.
My back was to her when she walked into the yard before
the temple, but I sensed she was behind me, and when I
turned to face her neither of us could find words. We
stared into each other's eyes a full minute before I remembered my manners and bowed in greeting. She was crying.
I tried desperately to speak to her, but the words would
not come.

"I understand," she said almost inaudibly, "I understand,
my son." She placed the bundle of food she had brought on
the ground near my feet. "I understand. The lonesome-
ness . . ."

Finally, I found my voice. "I would rather be alone," I
told her, "but I am not by myself. I am always with
Buddha."

There was nothing more to be said. Still crying, restrain-
ing from touching me, she turned away and started down
the mountain. I wanted to run to her then, to press myself
to her and be comforted. I wished I might again be Kimbo,
who led the boys in the village and played at war and
cleaned the sooty lamps and stretched to brush the dust
from the ceiling beams. But it wasn't a time to drown in
such display of emotion.

I watched until she was out of sight. Then I, too, wept.

I should have known that my mother would come to
see me. I had enjoyed a closeness with my mother when
I was a child. Only children do; and in the family of more
than one child, such as in mine, there is always a favorite.
It is usually the last born, the youngest, as in my case.

The visit from my mother, agonizing as it was for us
both, kindled thoughts of my family from which my soul
still fled. I pictured my brothers and sisters being divided
in their understanding of my actions by natural sibling
rivalry on the one hand, the relation of blood on the other.

I wondered about my sister's thoughts on what the old fortuneteller had said to me. "You will not become a navy officer . . . you will become successful and become better known than a navy officer." His prediction came back to mind. The first of it had come true. Now I puzzled over the second part—and the third. He had said I would go to a foreign country.

Of all my family, I wondered most about my father. My sense of the humiliation and dishonor my failure had caused him played a major role in my decision to kill myself. I felt my attempt at hara-kiri had disgraced me still further in his eyes.

Another month went by.

Eichi continued to visit me every fortnight. He followed my progress carefully, observing my increase in health, the sense of peace which gradually came to characterize my thoughts. After reviewing my routine he told me I might take a two hour nap in the afternoon, after lunch, to balance the strenuous exertions of mind and body to which I applied myself in the morning.

But I preferred to walk. Until they hid themselves away for the winter, I tried to make friends with the squirrels and other small animals who were my only company. I shared my rice with the birds. And out of the empathy developing in me, I spoke to them.

"You live in the wilderness, but I see you are happy, untouched by civilization. You are well fed by your own means. I love you as much as you love me, because you trust me, knowing I will not harm you. That is why you are here, why you come to take the handful of rice I offer. You accept it gladly, and that gives me great pleasure."

The birds paid no attention to my voice. They ate, pecking the grains of rice I scattered about my feet, and walking about me within reach—their heads bobbing, without fear. Their trust warmed my heart. I spoke to them as I wished I could speak to my mother and father.

Upon returning to the temple from an afternoon walk one day, I found my father waiting, sitting on the temple steps. As I approached, he got to his feet and extended his hand, not to grasp mine, but to give me a little gold and silver ornament taken from the scabbard of one of the swords in the family armory. The token represented the spirit of our honorable ancestors, the samurai of the past who fought for the Genji.

"You take it," he said. "Keep it."

The gift carried forgiveness with it. When my father spoke his voice was soft with understanding. I think it masked tears. But my father never cried. Never. His face could mirror sorrow—how well I knew the look—but tears never flushed his eyes. My memory of him is a memory of a strong man, resolute in mind and character, who spoke little, but with finality. I see him now at the long table at dinner time, drinking sake, smiling, observing, taking our measure as my brothers and sisters and I sat about him. His high position as governor earned him many invitations to be entertained at the teahouses. His position obliged him to go. But I remember he once remarked, during a silence at dinner one evening, "This is much better than having geisha girls about me."

I turned the sword ornament over in my hand, fondling it. Now I knew that my father understood, that mixed with his stern nature, his intense pride, and his adamant sense of power—as governor of Chiba and as head of his family—there was compassion.

After giving me the token, he left. I was alone again.

The winter came and went. Suddenly it was spring. The earth burst with new life. Once more the winds were warm, the sun golden and unmasked. The thick mists shrouding the mountain top drifted into oblivion. Below in the valley I could see fields being plowed. Far out at sea I saw the fishing boats, black specks rising and falling on the crest of the water.

Eichi came to see me more often after winter passed. We talked about my feelings and my studies. Now, when he asked me what I had learned, I could speak freely.

During one visit, he asked me, "What do you think of your body now? Do you respect it?"

"Yes."

"You know, at first I thought you might again give yourself over to irrational depression and hang yourself."

I laughed. For the first time in months, I laughed. Although melancholy had left me, I had not reacquired a sense of humor. "With what?" I exclaimed. "There is no rope here!"

"Then you considered the thought?"

"Not until you mentioned it. No, it never entered my mind."

"Better and better," Eichi said. He settled himself on the ground. "The solitude you put yourself in here at this old temple, the searching you made of your soul, the meditation, your exercise, what has all this brought you?"

"Peace," I told him. "If nothing else, peace." I placed my hand on my heart. "Here, and in my mind. My head is clearer now. I feel purged. I feel renewed hope. I don't know what the future holds in store, but it must hold something."

"Indeed it does. Have you noticed that every *koan* involves a dilemma of some sort; that generally there is a choice of two alternatives, both of which are equally impossible."

"Zen is a man hanging from a tree over a cliff," I quoted. "He is holding on to a twig with his teeth. His hands hold no branch. His feet find no branch. Up on the cliff-edge a man shouts at him: 'Why did Bodhidharma come from

India into China?' If he fails to answer he is lost. If he
answers, he dies. What must he do?"

Eichi pursed his lips and nodded. "The alternatives of
assertion and denial. Both obscure the truth. To Zen the
problem of life is to pass beyond these. Thus each *koan*
reflects the great *koan* of life.

"Buddha said, 'All that we are is a result of what we
have thought.' We are the sum of our deeds, what we have
done and what we have thought. Our deeds are karma, as
you know from your reading. Karma is 'that moral kernel
of any being which survives death and continues in trans-
migration.' "

"Karma is cause then?"

"Yes."

"My suffering—karma?"

"The effect of something you did—yes."

"I did nothing but try to achieve my ambition."

"Is this your only life? What of previous karma?"

"My intense desire to become a naval officer, strangled
by the outcome of my attempt to feed my ego—to win my
diving bet—resulted in crushing my ego."

"And you sought to balance the scale by hara-kiri," Eichi
interjected. "Perhaps. Perhaps the cause was evil karma
from before, unconsciously exerting its influence."

"Karma, then, will shape my future."

"No place exists on earth where a man can escape his
karma. You are still subject to karmic causation, and will
be for a long time. Enlightenment and entry into nirvana
will free you from the control of karma, but neither is
achieved overnight. You have made a good beginning, but
the law of cause and effect will govern you for a long time
to come.

"But remember, Kintaro, the deeds which are karma you
are free to choose."

"Why must the deeds be ones which cause no **suffering**?"

"Fulfillment in the way of Zen will take a long time. Years. You must study and meditate. But there must be action, too. You must practice what you learn. Put your trust in the four noble truths of Buddha: Suffering is universal; its cause is desire; when desire ceases, suffering ends; the way to end desire and suffering is by following the eight-fold path:

"Right thoughts, right mindfulness, right concentration, right resolution, right speech, right behavior, right effort, right vocation.

"Work to achieve the ten great perfections: generosity, goodness, renunciation, wisdom, firmness, patience, truth, resolution, kindness, equanimity."

I remained silent when he finished speaking. I thought about all he had said. I sat as if in a trance. Minutes passed. Then, suddenly, I became aware of Eichi rising to his feet. I looked up at him. "When should I return?" I asked.

"That is for you and you only to decide."

Once more I watched him disappear into the trees, following the narrow path down the mountainside.

It was May, in the fullness of spring. I had gone to sit where I could watch the ships leaving and entering Tokyo Bay. As I watched the ocean, it came to me how far the water stretched, touching Japan and extending to touch Australia and America. I was thinking, "If one puts something in the water here, it's bound to reach anyone, anywhere."

As I sat thinking, watching the water, a large passenger boat came into view, bound for Yokohama. It glided toward the mouth of Tokyo Bay. Suddenly, I realized it **was** moving too close to the shore! I wondered if it would hit the rocks—the shoals lurking just beneath the glistening **surface** of the water.

I watched the ship drift closer to the shore, to where what the Nanaura fishermen call Devil's Rock was waiting. The ship must have been a full mile from me, but I began calling, trying to warn it away, screaming at the captain: "Go back! Go back!"

But the ship continued to come.

I waved and jumped up and down like a madman. I pressed my fists to my temples and tried to concentrate on thinking the ship out of danger. I was powerless, of course. The ship slowly plunged into Devil's Rock and stopped, listing to one side.

The next moment found me running down the mountainside. My thoughts of Zen, of self, were gone, submerged in my desire to help those on the stricken ship. I thought of nothing else until I reached my father's house and stood before him.

"There is a ship," I faltered, "wrecked in the channel. The people . . ."

"It is the *Dakota*, a steamship from the United States," my father said.

Time did not allow explanation. "I must go to help," I said.

"Not only must you, I command you to do so," my father replied. "Take the bicycle and go. Do all that you can do."

I knew that I would be of some help, for I spoke English —not well, but I had studied it in school. I rushed from the house and rode to the village to organize for the rescue. Only later, when I was weary from the work, did I realize that I had at last returned to the world of men.

4   Return to the World of Men

I PEDALED FURIOUSLY TO THE SHORE OPPOSITE THE STRICKEN
ship. The sea between was alive with fishing boats engaged
in taking off the passengers, twelve hundred in all.

In my dash to participate in the rescue, I forgot about
Zen. My concern was not for myself, but for those in need.
For humanity. I suppose that might be called part of Zen,
but I never considered it in that light. I just obeyed the
order of my heart and went to give my help.

No one was injured or killed, just shaken up and scared.
The beach was dotted with groups of passengers, huddled
together, cut off from their rescuers by a language barrier.
There they sat, some soaked to the skin, all shocked by the
abrupt, near-tragic end to their journey.

Without explanation, I began to give orders. To organize. Food and shelter were the obvious problems to solve.
In short order, the school was converted into a dormitory,

74

blankets were gathered by the armload, the passengers were divided among the families with houses which could take them. Perhaps a hundred of the passengers were directed to the local Buddhist temple.

I was the only one in the village who could speak English, and so I was in demand everywhere at once to interpret and explain. I found myself going from house to house, from the temple to the two small hotels in the village, answering questions, giving orders, reassuring, explaining. At one point, a group of young girls, in their late teens, attracted me. I think I paid them more attention. And was embarrassed the most by them. They asked me where they could go to the toilet. I could do nothing but flush beet red and point.

Providing food for the passengers turned out to be a hilarious undertaking. I organized what one passenger later referred to as "the great chicken hunt." All the chickens in the village and around it were gathered, along with hundreds of eggs, bags and bags of rice, soy sauce and salt. For five days, until a rescue ship arrived from Yokohama, the passengers ate chicken, boiled eggs, rice and chicken soup. Great pots of food were carried from house to house. When it was over, there wasn't a chicken to be had in Nanaura. Every time someone mentioned chicken we burst out laughing. I'm sure that a great number of people lost their taste for chicken after five straight days of it.

The gratitude of the passengers and the crew of the *Dakota* was immense. They offered to pay for everything, but my father refused. He believed it his duty and privilege to bear the cost. He paid for all the food.

Participating in the rescue gave me a chance to talk with many people. For the first time I saw something of the world outside Japan. The captain and many of the passengers told me about America. They urged me to go there.

To go and study there. Again and again I was urged to "Visit the United States, Mr. Hayakawa. If you do, please be sure to get in touch." Many of the passengers gave me cards bearing their names and addresses. But, later, I threw them all away. I thought then there was no reason to go to America. What I had to study I was studying up on the mountain. I didn't want to go to America, but I did think about it. The idea of going slowly began to grow in my mind. And once more, the prediction of the fortuneteller returned: "You will not stay in Japan. You will travel across the waters."

When the rescue ship from Yokohama came for the passengers of the *Dakota*, I was asked to return to Yokohama with them. I went there with them, and to Tokyo, interpreting for them, and listening to their stories of life in the United States and why I should go there.

"You seem to be quite bright," one passenger said to me. "You speak English fairly well. You seem in command of yourself. What do you plan to do here in Japan?"

In command of myself? What could I say about that? I told him I had once studied for a naval career. "But that is over," I said. "I really have no plans for the future at the moment."

"Then why not go? Surely your father, the governor, can send you. Go to America and study. Lord knows, you're serious enough. Don't you ever smile?"

Americans are so blunt, I thought. So different from us Japanese. In reply to his question, I grinned.

After I returned to Nanaura from Tokyo, I began to think about visiting America. All that I had seen and heard began to exert an influence. The talk of the passengers tumbled around in my head. Suddenly I wanted to go to America, to see it for myself!

Very little was said by my family about my return from

the temple on the mountainside. I like to think that my show of desire to help others was all the explanation necessary. My family took me back. That was the main thing. My father did not speak about what had happened to me before, nor did he mention anything about what he felt I should do now.

The *Dakota* hit Devil's Rock in May, 1909. Nearly eighteen months had passed since I was expelled from the navy. The months were the hardest I had ever spent. But now I was back home, ready to begin anew. But begin what? I asked myself. If not a life of retreat on the mountain, then what?

The more I thought about America, the more I wanted to go there. Somewhere, deep within me, burned the natural human desire to prove myself, to make something of myself. Perhaps the selflessness of aiding the passengers of the *Dakota* had relighted the flame. I don't know. But the urge was there. The months I spent at the old temple had begun to lighten the darkness.

I puzzled over cause and effect. Perhaps it was meant to be—this sudden flight back to the world of men from the content I was finding in my pursuit of self. Why did the ship strike the rock? Why did I see it? Why did I instantly rush to help total strangers? What karma were governing me now?

A week or so after the rescue ship from Yokohama had come and gone, and the *Dakota* itself had been repaired and refloated, I made mention at dinner that I wished to go to America. My father was thunderstruck!

"Absolutely out of the question," he said.

"But why? I want to go. I want to."

"To do what?"

"To see for myself."

My father raised his hands from his sides and let them

fall to rest on his knees. "There you have it," he said, leaning toward me slightly. "To see for yourself. What will it prove?"

"I do not intend to prove anything, Father, except to myself that there is something more than Japan. Do you expect me to remain here for the rest of my life and raise rice, perhaps? Or perhaps fish? I . . ."

"You are insolent! I have given my decision. You are not going to America."

I had poured and drank sake continually while we argued. Now I did so with angry abandon. "Then I will go to Hokkaido! I will go to the mines like the rest of the thick-headed hairy northerners!"

My father glared at me savagely. "You will leave us. You have had too much sake."

"Perhaps I have not had enough!" I began to raise my voice and slap the table between us with the flat of my hands.

"Kimbo, please." It was my mother who spoke. "Do as your father says. We will talk of your wish later."

"There is nothing more to be discussed," my father said sharply.

My mother did not appear to hear him. "Later," she said to me. "Now go."

As I left the room I heard my father lay down his law to my mother. He spoke with icy calm. "I am master here, and I say no. He will not go to America. And he will not be so foolish as to go to the mines in Hokkaido. The mines at Hokkaido! What sort of threat is that?"

My mother's response was an unintelligible murmur. I could not hear her. But my father's words echoed after me. "When I say no, I mean no. There is a place for him here."

I left the house and went into the garden to work off my anger by throwing sticks for Kame.

A day or two passed. Nothing more was said about my desire to go to America until, once again at the end of the evening meal, it became the topic of conversation. Then it was my father who spoke first.

"Your mother is most persuasive, Kintaro. It seems I am not completely master here," he said. He smiled. "My mind was made up, but it has been changed. You may go to America."

"Father, I . . ."

He held up his hand. "Let me finish. You may go, but with a purpose. I want you to study while you are there. Inasmuch as I am in government service, I have made it my business to become familiar with political science, both here in Japan and elsewhere. I want you to study political science." He looked at me, then at my mother. She sat silent, a slight smile of deference curving her lips. I looked at her and thought: You never change, you are always the same. I smiled and turned back to my father.

"I'm sure you feel that there is no time like the present," he went on, "so plans best be made."

"It is something I must do, Father. Thank you. I hope you will forgive my rash outburst—what I said the other evening."

"The heat of anger boils reason. Besides, who can see clearly through the mists of sake? Thank your mother, Kintaro. I may rule Chiba Prefecture, but she appears to rule me." He sighed. "Your wish is to go to America. Her wish is that you get yours. What can I do?" He paused to sip from his cup of sake. "But make no mistake. I do not send you there to sate yourself with the pleasures America offers. You are to study and study hard. I will make arrangements for you to enter the University of Chicago. A Professor Jennings teaches there. Political economics. I think highly of him."

"Chicago?"

"It is like Tokyo, big and busy. Cosmopolitan, I believe is the term."

Within the week I found myself gone from Nanaura to the peninsula port of Tateyama, where I caught a small steamship, a coaster, which took me to Yokohama and the ocean liner I traveled on to the United States.

My departure from my parents and Nanaura was like that of some Genji lord of old leaving to do battle. I said goodbye to my father and mother the night before the morning I left.

"Kintaro," my father said, "remember when you were a little boy, a small boy, first in grammar school. You chased a thief with a knife, not thinking he was a man and you were a child. You showed great courage, great spirit. Don't forget that spirit. All that has happened is over. Look to the future. Study and make a success of yourself. If people do something bad to you, return it double. However, if people do something nice to you, return it threefold. This is the way of life to me."

Pausing for a moment, my father went to a carved chest against the wall at the far end of the room. He returned with two ornate swords, a long one such as used in battle and *kendo*, and a short sword, the sort used for hara-kiri. He handed these to me, saying, "Take these with you and think of them as men's souls."

The swords were the only treasures I carried with me. The gift of them symbolized trust and inspiration. They stood for strength and goodness of character. It was for me to live up to the reputation.

"Strive to succeed," my father went on. "It is not simple. But make your mark!" His voice suddenly rose. For a moment he was not my father, sad that I was leaving, but the governor of Chiba, imperious and stern. "Stay ten years! Do not come back until you have made your mark in the world!" Having said this, the expression of authority faded from his face and he was my father again. When I looked into his eyes, they glistened. But no tears came. His gaze on me was soft and benign. "Say goodbye to your mother," he said, and, under his breath, I heard him tell himself, "Ten years. In ten years I shall be eighty."

While my father spoke to me, my mother sat, her head bent, watching her hands. She was peeling me a pear, slowly drawing her sharp small paring knife through the thin skin. When I turned to her, I noticed for the first time that her hair was white. Until that moment, I had not really noticed. Suddenly, I realized how old she and my father were. My father was seventy, my mother not much younger.

Seeing the white of my mother's hair impressed me vividly. Later that night, when I was alone, about to sleep my last hours in my father's house, that impression compelled me to take brush, ink, and rice paper and compose a *haiku*, a refined form of Japanese poem which, in Japanese, consists of seventeen syllables. In Zen, a success at *haiku* is looked upon as an expression of temporary *satori*. I wrote:

> Mother, who is peeling the pear for me,
> The night before the farewell;
> It is the first time I notice
> Her hair turning white.

The night passed. I awoke and rose at five in the morning. Breakfast with my parents was solemn and wordless. My father had made all arrangements. My passport, tickets and some money were tucked in my pocket. For my trip, I had bought an English-style suit; it was not my custom, but it would hardly do for me to travel to and arrive in America wearing a kimono and sandals.

After breakfast, my father walked with me to the gate of his house. He had a horse and carriage waiting to take me to Tateyama. My mother walked behind us. At the gate, I put down the white Chinese suitcase I was carrying, turned to my parents and bowed low, bending from the waist, my hands on my knees slipping lower as I bent in honor and affection. We did not kiss or clasp hands. I straightened, took up my bag and climbed into the carriage. In the remaining few moments before the driver slapped the reins on the horse's rump I looked at my father.

"This is the last time I will see you, Kintaro," he said. He closed his eyes and turned away as the carriage started to move.

As my carriage rolled through the village toward the public road to Tateyama, people began to appear in doorways and at the roadside. Word of my departure had reached the village, and in spite of the early hour, the farmers, fishers and others turned out to see me leave. They bowed, and each time I descended from the carriage to bow in return.

I reached Tateyama shortly after six o'clock, and boarded the small coastal steamship for the six-hour trip to Yokohama. It stopped at ports along the peninsula five or six times before reaching Tokyo and then proceeding to Yokohama. There I had my last personal contact with home and family. Without my knowing, Tora, the deaf and dumb friend of my childhood, and Hisataro, the hunchback, had journeyed to Yokohama ahead of me and were waiting when I arrived there. They had come to see me safely on board the liner which would take me to the United States. The *Aki-maru*, it was named.

Both Tora and Hisataro, crying, fell upon my neck. "This is the last time we will see you," Tora signaled, his fingers flying in the sign language I had taught him. I had also taught him to write and to know the name of each man in Nanaura.

"I don't think so," I assured them. "I shall be back. In ten years—twelve, perhaps—I shall return and will see you."

They followed me to the lighter which took me out to the ship riding at anchor in the channel. The last I saw of them, they were bowing and waving, both crying, standing on the dock.

The *Aki-maru* did not sail until a few days later. Then, late in the afternoon, while I was getting ready to have dinner, the parting whistle was blown and we got under way toward the mouth of Tokyo Bay. I ate dinner quickly and went out on deck. The course of the ship took her around the end of the Boso Peninsula and past the Nanaura coast out into the open sea. We came abreast of the village at about seven o'clock in the evening. The last light of the sun was fading from the sky. It was hazy. But as I stood at the rail and peered at the shore I could see two large bonfires burning; one on the beach, the other up on the mountain behind Nanaura. My brother wrote me later that the fire on the beach was a farewell fire lit at my father's direction. The one on the mountain, blazing out of the falling night, had been lit by Tora and Hisataro. As I watched, my father's last words rang in my ears. "This is the last time I will see you, Kintaro." I began to cry.

There is a Buddhist saying: "Meeting is the beginning of departure." Meeting people is the beginning of departure, because when you meet, afterward you will part, sooner or later. Departure is always sad. I thought as I watched the fires that from the day I was born I had been departing from my family and friends. Now, in fact, I had. Looking at the fires, it struck me that they were funeral fires. That night, alone on deck, I fought a battle with emotion and lost. Zen had put a measure of content in my heart and strength in my mind, but it could not steel me against the sorrow that always accompanies parting from loved ones. Even the eyes of a stoic grow misty at such a time. As my father's eyes did. In the darkness, as Japan fell behind in the wake of the ship, with only the sea to witness, I cried until I could cry no more.

The following morning, I awoke suddenly, startled into consciousness by the roll and pitch of the *Aki-maru* as it steamed northward to take the Great Circle Route to Seattle, some fourteen days before us. I dressed, breakfasted and went out on deck to set about meeting my fellow passengers. It was a glorious day, sunny and warm.

Almost immediately, I fell in with a newspaperman. He was going to take a position as an American correspondent for a paper in Tokyo. To amuse ourselves and the other passengers we decided to publish a daily newspaper—a one-page affair for which we both reported. He composed and lettered the stories, and I drew pictures. Each edition was produced entirely by hand.

Among the passengers of the *Aki-maru* that I interviewed for our little newspaper were four girls about the same age as I—twenty, perhaps younger—who were en route to marry Japanese men living in the United States. The marriages had been arranged by correspondence. All the girls knew of the men they would marry was what was said in letters and conveyed by photographs. Picture brides, the girls were called. According to plan, they would be wed to their intendeds on the ship, by the captain, as soon as it reached Seattle.

The girls and their prospective husbands had been brought together by arrangements made by their parents and friends who acted as intermediaries. For some families in Japan this was the one sure way of assuring a daughter's future.

The four picture brides were very friendly and fun-loving. One of them, a very sweet, naïve nineteen-year-old from one of the islands of southern Japan, confided her excitement to me and showed me a picture of the man to whom she was promised. He seemed pleasant enough in appearance. But then, I couldn't tell very much from the picture, for it was greatly retouched.

When the *Aki-maru* docked at Seattle, the four picture brides were gathered in a tight little group at the rail, each peering down into the crowd on the pier, looking for her prospective mate. I watched them, amused as they jabbed and poked one another, giggling and laughing. The ship churned to a stop and the gangway was let down. The bridegrooms were practically the first ones aboard. I shifted my gaze elsewhere for a moment. When I again looked at the girls, one was missing.

The captain of the *Aki-maru* performed the wedding ceremony for three of the couples. The girls left the ship newly wed, newly come to a new country. I wondered where the fourth girl was.

"Mr. Hayakawa?" A steward suddenly appeared on deck calling my name. "Please follow me, sir. The captain would like to see you," he said when he found me. I went with him to the captain's quarters, where that officer drew me to one side to explain: "The last girl—the man is waiting. When she saw him come up the gangway, she burst into tears and bolted as if she had seen a demon. You interviewed her for your little newspaper during the voyage. You are close to her age. Perhaps she will confide in you. Find her and learn what's happened. I'll make up some excuse for him." He gestured toward the inner room of his quarters and the man waiting there, dressed in his Sunday best.

I said I would try, and went to the girl's cabin. It was empty. I turned to leave. Then I heard sobbing coming from the bathroom. I found the girl there, slumped on her knees against the wall, crying bitterly. "Why?" I asked. "The captain is waiting to perform the marriage ceremony."

"I can't marry him," she choked through her tears. "I can't. He deceived me. He . . ." She fumbled in her pocket for a moment and withdrew the man's photograph and thrust it at me. "He is not the same. He is older, and his face . . ."

I had seen the man come up the gangway. He was older than he appeared to be in the picture. His face was pock-marked.

"I will not marry him," she said. "I will go back to Japan without leaving the ship."

I stood looking at her, seeing her tear-stained face, for a moment dreaming her dream of happiness in America with her, and my heart went out to her. She had visualized wedded bliss with a handsome husband, a happy home, comfort and security. Now an ugly shatterer of her dream had come to claim her. I told her to wait for me, and went back to talk to the captain.

"What can you do in a case like this?" I asked him.

He shrugged and spread the fingers of his hands. "We've had a few experiences like this before," he said. "Worse than this one, in fact. Sometimes the picture is retouched, sometimes the picture is of another man entirely. That happened twice. Both girls went back rather than marry."

"But this is the same man."

"In false feathers, yes," the captain said. "What can you tell her?"

"What sort of a man is he? Do you know?"

"A little. I know he doesn't gamble or drink. He has a good business and will make good provision for her, I think."

"Well," I said, "I'll tell her something. She has my pity."

I returned to the girl's cabin. Her tears were gone. She sat on the edge of her bed waiting—hoping, I guess—for me to advise her.

"Does his appearance really mean so much to you?" I asked. "How much does it count in the happiness of your heart, against tenderness and understanding? I believe this man will try his best to make you happy. Whatever the look of his face, his heart is good and his character is noble. The captain speaks very well of him."

Years later, after I had come to know English sayings like "Beauty is only skin deep" and "Never judge a book by its cover," I thought of what I told this girl.

"Give him a chance," I urged her. "Give yourself a chance. Ask about his reputation. Study him and get to know him. Stay ten days and get to know him. If you find him to be as you think now, you have a perfect right to return to Japan. But he is a man who will make you happy, I think. Reserve judgment ten days. If he proves to be all you have dreamed of in every way but looks, then marry him. There is more to love than handsomeness and beauty."

I let my heart speak to her. I tried to share with her the contentment I had fought so hard to achieve. Finally, she consented to stay.

I saw that she washed her face, and went with her to the captain. "Look this man full in the face," I told her as we made our way along the corridor. "Do not embarrass him. He will be ashamed as it is when he learned you are not to be married right away."

Seattle was just a short stop for me. I only stayed there a day or so before taking another ship down the coast to San Francisco. Before I left Seattle I saw that this girl was registered at a dependable hotel. I confided in the proprietor and asked him to watch out for her. Later on, after the ten days I asked her to give the ugly man were up, I wrote to the proprietor of the hotel. I was curious and wanted to know how things had turned out. "I know the man quite well," he replied. "He is a good man, of good reputation. She gave him fair trial and he proved himself. The ceremony is over. They are married, and she is very happy. Very cheerful."

That was the last of the incident as far as it concerned me. I had since taken the ship south to San Francisco and gone east by train to Chicago to begin my studies at the university.

5   Omen of Destiny

"FRANKLY, MR. HAYAKAWA, YOU AND YOUR FRIEND HERE
would do well to wait until morning before disembarking."
   The captain of the steamship on which I traveled from
Seattle to San Francisco offered this advice. We reached
the city by the Golden Gate at midnight. I got my first
glimpse of San Francisco when, at slow speed, the ship
glided through a thin late evening fog and slipped into her
berth a few piers east of the famous Ferry Building that
stands like a sentinel at the waterside on the Embarcadero
at the foot of Market Street. Above us on its hills most of
the city lay in darkness.
   "I don't want to put the damper on your desire to put
your feet on land and begin seeing a bit of the country,"
the captain said, "but the San Francisco waterfront at night
is no church picnic. Morning should be soon enough. Stay
on board."

The captain was a bluff, friendly fellow who had my welfare at heart, I'm sure. He had made a point of introducing himself soon after I boarded the ship at Seattle. He seemed genuinely interested in the fact I had come all the way from Japan to attend the university in Chicago.

The friend the captain included in his advice to me was a young Japanese. He and I were the only Japanese to make the trip down from Seattle, and our nationality had immediately drawn us together. He was one of those young, enterprising Japanese who take quickly to Western ways. He was in the candle exporting business and had been in the United States some ten years. He was cocky, but affable, nonetheless. Although we did not discuss the subject at length, he told me he was *yodan*, or fourth rank in judo, and entitled to wear the black belt which is symbolic of a proficiency in the art. *Shichidan*, or seventh rank, is the highest designation of accomplishment one can achieve in judo. Very few men attain this rank. From it, the ranks decline to sixth, fifth, fourth and so on. I had studied judo from childhood, and by the time I was graduated from the Naval Preparatory School, I was third rank. I had since progressed to fourth.

"I don't think we need worry," my friend told the captain. "I know San Francisco fairly well. We plan on going to a Japanese hotel, the Kumamoto, by carriage."

Eager to get going, I followed his lead. I got my luggage together, and with him went down the gangway and climbed into one of a number of horse-drawn hacks that had met the ship. We started off at a fast trot down the Embarcadero, away from what light there was at the pier, into the foggy darkness. I yelled to the driver to slow down, but he paid no attention. Finally, about a mile from the ship, the hack slowed. A man ran up and jumped to stand on the side entry step. Before my friend and I could say anything, the hack was stopped and the driver was waving a pistol at us.

"Whatever you have, we'll take," the driver said.

I reached inside my jacket for my money, and while doing so whispered to my friend in Japanese, "Get the other man, I'll get the driver. Now!" I exhorted, and lunged forward chopping my right hand down to knock the pistol out of the driver's hand. He gave a yell in pain and grabbed for his wrist. I clamped my left hand around his wrist, brought my right up under his elbow and levered him end over end out of the hack. He lit on his back on the bricks of the street, sprawled and lay still. Before I could take a breath, his companion was on me. He dragged me from the hack and drew back an arm to hit me. When he let fly, I dodged and used his own momentum to throw him as well.

With both men lying unconscious at my feet, I looked for my friend. He was gone. I called, but got no answer. For something close to an hour I stood in the dim light of the side lamp of the hack holding the pistol on the two men who had tried to rob us. My fourth-rank friend finally returned bringing two policemen. One took our assailants to jail; the other, a tall, heavily built Negro, saw us safely to the Kumamoto Hotel.

This was my welcome to San Francisco: attempted robbery! My thoughts about America were now mixed. I was not so naïve as to think there were no criminals in the United States; I just didn't think misfortune began the moment you set foot in the country. As for my shipboard friend, we parted company when we went to our rooms at the hotel.

The attempted robbery was my first surprise in America. The Negro policeman was my second. I had read about the plight of the Negro before and after the Civil War

when I was in school. The following morning, when I left
the hotel to take my first real look at San Francisco, I was
compelled to stop and ask a passer-by, "Are the Negro
policemen here only for Negroes?" "For everybody." The
reply surprised me. I still thought of Negroes as mis-
treated, downtrodden, with few rights and privileges.

San Francisco, that summer of 1909, was still scarred by
the effects of the earthquake and fire that had all but killed
her three years before. But it was then as it is now, a
beautiful city. As I walked about it, sight-seeing, I was
amazed at seeing so many buildings of stone and brick.
Although the cities of Japan were not all paper, bamboo
and wood in the early 1900's, they could not match San
Francisco's architectural strength.

"She's quite the place to see," the captain of the ship
had told me during one of our conversations. "Not as large
as Chicago, where you're going, of course; but more of a
treat for the eyes. Too bad we'll be pulling in so late at
night. Nothing like a view of San Francisco from the bay."

I had admired his pride. Nonetheless, I tried to picture
Tokyo and Yokohama for him.

I wandered around San Francisco until my legs ached,
but I stayed away from the waterfront. I was not about to
tempt fate a second time. Still, if it had been my destiny to
be robbed and perhaps murdered, such would have been.
But judo had saved me, and the presence of mind given
me by Zen practice had welled my courage. The demand
of the moment left me little time in which to think. Once
the threat was made, my mind and body responded instantaneously. Such readiness and quickness is the result of
long concentration in Zen practice. Zen is a religion of
compassion, but part of what it gives the self identified
with the human being is a presence of mind which pre-

cludes fear. When the physical being is threatened, protection is the immediate reaction; and the reaction takes
place without intellection. To stop to think might well tip
the scales the other way.

Of course, to possess this facility does not imply one is
perpetually on guard—wary and suspicious. To exist in
such a state makes conscious caution obligatory. In Zen
the state is a matter of the super-conscious resulting from
the development of another sense of intuition.

First impressions are lasting ones. Those I had of San
Francisco: the arrival by ship in the fog at midnight, the
attempted robbery, the Negro policeman—these, and one
other, have remained fresh.

The other impression was the appalling effect seeing so
many tall American women had on me. I am five and a
half feet in height. Many of the women I saw on the streets
of San Francisco as I walked around the city wore low-
heeled boots which buttoned up the sides. Even so, they
were much taller than I. Vanity has no place in Zen, but
just the same I have been a long time losing the self-
consciousness a taller woman brings out in a man shorter
than herself. The first tall woman I saw made me think
how terrible it would be to have one as my wife.

I went by train from San Francisco to Chicago, traveling
up and over the craggy, forest-laden Sierra Nevada Mountains, across the desert wasteland of Nevada to Salt Lake
City, Utah. There the train made a half-hour stop on the
first morning of what was then a three-day trip.

The short stop in Salt Lake City was a welcome one. I
left the train to walk and stretch my legs. I attracted
attention immediately, being the only Japanese among the
crowd of passengers which streamed into the station from
the train to purchase newspapers, magazines, coffee and,

in spite of the early hour, something someone later explained to me was sarsaparilla—a sweet drink which totally mystified my taste buds when I first tried it.

People, how they conduct themselves and why they act as they do, and what they have to say, have always been of great interest to me. I say this because most people, particularly in the Western world, consider Japanese to be reticent and introspective, of the world, but not in it. I myself enjoy making friends and having a good time in the midst of pleasant companions.

Gregarious social intercourse did not blossom until later in my life, however; I met only two people during the train trip—two elderly businessmen from the Middle West who stopped by my seat in the day coach to exude a sort of friendliness called, I think, corn-fed. Like the captain of the ship in San Francisco, they were very much interested in what I was going to do in the United States.

I also made one other acquaintance, in the railroad station in Salt Lake City. I struck up a conversation with the assistant stationmaster and we talked until it was time for my train to go. Later, when the demands of acting often took me to New York and back to Hollywood, I saw and talked with him every time my train stopped there.

These three persons and the San Francisco ship captain—totally different from one another—gave me my first look into the national character of a people whose subsequent appreciation helped make me the success the old fortune-teller in Nanaura had foretold I would be. During their brief contacts with me they were unselfish in their kindness. Such selflessness is part of Zen. It produces karma of far-reaching good effect.

The remainder of my train trip to Chicago was a wearisome rolling across the barren land of Wyoming, through the long stretches of Nebraska and Iowa farmlands. Despite the newness of things to see, I grew bored and restless. But the breadth of the country amazed me, as it must amaze all foreigners who visit the United States, many of whose homelands are at most a day's train journey from border to border. It astounded me even more when I realized that another thousand miles of American civilization reached eastward beyond Chicago to New York.

When I arrived at Chicago, I went directly from the railroad station to the university where, in short order, I was enrolled, assisted in planning a program of study and aided in locating a suitable place to live. Fortunately, my ability to speak English kept me from having to take the special preparatory language course the University of Chicago required of the foreign students who came to be educated there.

It was late June when I arrived at the university. When the Fourth of July came I was invited to a large dinner party, at which I was singled out to speak. What I said has been said a million times, I suspect. I talked about the organization of the Congress and the election of George Washington to the presidency. I was petrified when I did it, but, happily, my speech revealed my command of English and helped me integrate more swiftly into university life.

I made the first of my life-long American friends while I was at the University of Chicago, William Connery, whose father then owned the company which supplied most of the coal burned in Chicago furnaces and stoves.

As a youth in college, Bill Connery was very peculiar. He was highly pessimistic. I found his attitude strange for a son of a millionaire who rarely wanted for anything material. His was an attitude totally contrary to mine. Consequently, we became close friends. He saw darkness where I saw light. My detachment from all that plagued him, fascinated him. We had many long talks on philosophy together.

"This Zen you speak of, Kintaro," he asked me, "does it actually lie at the heart of your self-dominance?" Nothing appeared to bother or upset me. He couldn't understand it. "These guys," he said one day, referring to some of the other students, "they call you Jap and hara-kiri while they draw their hands across their bellies, and you—you just pass it all off! My god! Don't you ever get mad?"

"Why get mad?" I asked. "They mean no harm. I would know if they did."

"Doesn't it hurt your feelings?"

"Bill," I told him, "to trouble myself about it is to invite conflict—controversy. For what? I pity them in their ignorance. Perhaps someday, when their minds are broader, they may realize the infantile cruelty of what they say and the condescending attitude they display."

"Uh-huh." That's all he would say. "Uh-huh."

"I try to be objective about it."

"No wonder they think you're such a cold fish," he commented.

I laughed. His subjective emotions were always so near the surface. No wonder he was pessimistic. His attitude invited conflict.

What I had learned from Zen helped me a great deal in my relationships in college. Being a stranger was extremely difficult. Human nature being what it is, a stranger is always suspect. People fear what they do not understand, and move to defend themselves whether threat is apparent or not. I was something of a novelty at the university. During my first month or two there I provoked curiosity everywhere I went. To the insults I was handed, I paid little attention. I never disliked their source, or got angry; I just smiled and promptly forgot. The insult passed and was gone. Forgetting what is past is high virtue. I countered insults with friendliness, and usually won. More often than not, the student who heckled me rudely one day

made a point of stepping forward and shaking my hand a
few days later.

My years at the university were most uneventful. During
summer vacations I worked as an iceman, traveling to take
jobs in Salt Lake City, Atlantic City and at various vacation
spots around Chicago. My family and I corresponded
regularly. My father sent me the money I needed for living
when I attended classes; the extra money for the amuse-
ments of dining out, attending the theater and the motion
pictures, I earned carrying ice. I did not have a girl friend.
Girls didn't interest me then.

But athletics did. My second year at college, I went out
for football.

"The football team!" When Bill Connery and my other
friends learned of my intention they hooted and roared.
"But, Kintaro," Bill exclaimed, "you only weigh—what, a
hundred pounds?"

"A hundred and thirty-two."

Bill struggled to keep a straight face. "What position are
you going to play?" he asked.

"Tackle."

"Tackle? You? You're too light!"

"I don't see where my joining the football team is so
strange," I remarked. "There is a gentleman at Harvard
who weighs a hundred thirty-five pounds and plays a very
good game."

Bill shook his head. Undaunted, I conscientiously
attended practice and studied to understand the game. I
admit that the coach expressed grave doubts about my
fitness to play, but he let me try, nevertheless. I did very
well. No matter how big a man came at me in blocking
practice, upon contact he wound up flat on the field, out
of play. I simply employed *taiatari*, judo body technique.

After my first real game, it was noised about the campus
that I possessed occult power.

But a good thing can't last. The second season I played,

the members of an opposing team complained. The use of judo or jujitsu was promptly forbidden. Once and a while thereafter, however, in the heat of the game I would forget; and after the University of Chicago varsity was penalized ten and fifteen yards four or five times, I was put off the team.

So much for football. I enjoyed playing the game very much, albeit my special way; and confess that I did better at it than in some of my studies. I had little trouble with political science, but the fundamentals of economics baffled me.

"Something has happened to your father." These words came into my mind one evening during my junior year, when I sat alone in my room studying. I had stopped for a moment to sharpen my pencil. The knife slipped and I cut a finger. I can't explain why, but when this happened I wrote the time and date on a slip of paper and tucked it away in my desk drawer.

Not long afterward, I received a pile of letters from home. Four or five came from my brothers and sisters, but one bore a different postmark. I opened that letter first. It was from a friend. He was studying at Kyushu and wrote to me in English.

"Kimbo, my friend, I know how you must feel. The news of your father saddened me, too. I hope you will accept my condolences. He was a good man, a just governor. I am here at the university studying . . ." The letter trailed off on other subjects.

I read the other letters. One by one I went through them. They contained nothing that would explain my friend's expression of sympathy. Obviously, my father was dead, but my family had kept the news from me. I reread my friend's letter. He is mistaken, I thought. I took the letter to Professor Jennings, my political economics instructor, but, regretfully, he confirmed what I read was true.

"Then my father will never know I have fulfilled his wish here," I said. I took back the letter and returned to my room to look at the time and date I had jotted down the night I cut my finger. At that moment I had received a premonition of tragedy. I had known then! But I had dismissed the thought from my mind.

I did not tell my family that I knew my father was dead, but let them think their secret was being kept. I continued my studies, and in June 1913 was graduated a Bachelor of Arts. Bill Connery and a few other friends and the Japanese Consul stationed in Chicago were in the audience when I walked across the stage in mortarboard and robe to receive my diploma.

"Well?" Bill asked me following the ceremonies.

"Well, what?"

"What are you going to do now?"

"Go back to Japan and into politics, I guess. That's what I studied here for."

"I'll miss you, Kintaro. All the good times."

"We have been parting from the moment we met," I said.

"More of the Buddha stuff, huh?"

I nodded and gripped his hand. "It is time for me to go. I'm taking the train to Los Angeles tomorrow."

In Los Angeles I had a few days to wait before my ship sailed for Japan. I relaxed and went sight-seeing, visiting Little Tokyo, the Japanese settlement there.

One afternoon, a day or so after I arrived, I stopped to have a slice of cantaloupe being sold from a pushcart by an old man in the Little Tokyo section. The old man stared at me as I stood on the sidewalk eating.

"Excuse me," he said when I was nearly finished, "but I perceive you are not a man from around here." He was very polite in his speech, speaking as he looked, like a patriarch advisor to some noble family. "You are different."

"I just recently arrived in town from Chicago," I told him. "I graduated from the university there."

"I don't mean that you are not a local man," he replied. "I mean you are not a man of this earth. I don't know what your name is, but I see it written in the sky."

"You joke, old man," I said, laughing.

His face clouded. "No, I don't. I don't know you, and I can't explain why I have told you what I have. But your face, the look of it so struck me. I have seen such a cast of expression only one other time."

The old man stared as he talked. His eyes seemed to lose their fixedness then, and for a time he appeared to be in a trance. "Years ago, when I was traveling in Hiroshima," he said, "I met two young men—students they said they were—one poorly dressed, the other obviously the son of a rich family. The shabby one—the look of his face—compelled me to speak to him as I have spoken to you. I saw the mark of greatness on him and told him so. He later rose to be Minister of State."

I snorted at this and tossed the rind from the piece of melon I had eaten into a bucket swinging from a nail at one end of the pushcart. "Preposterous nonsense," I said. I continued my walk.

"You must believe," the old man insisted as I moved away. "In the sky . . . I see your name written in the sky."

The evening before I was to sail home to Japan from San Pedro, the seaport for Los Angeles, and take up a career in politics and government, I chose to celebrate a little by attending a performance at the Japanese Theatre. It was a small playhouse dedicated to bringing a dramatic breath of their homeland to those living in Little Tokyo. The theatre was operated and the plays produced by a man named Toyo Fujita. I went prepared to spend a pleasant evening among my own and was unpleasantly bored beyond belief. The play—I have long forgotten the title—was trite in plot and poorly acted. The performance tried my patience to such a point that when it ended I marched around to the stage door and demanded to see the manager.

I returned the bow of the confident man who approached me and promptly launched my criticism: "I saw the play tonight and it was something out of the bottom of the barrel."

"I beg your pardon."

"I should think if you had an eye for success and profit you would offer something besides old chestnuts. I'd sooner sit through an evening of *haiku*."

Mr. Fujita ran an appraising eye over me. "I suppose you can do better, Mr. . . ."

"Hayakawa. Kintaro Hayakawa." We shook hands. "Yes, I can!" I boasted impetuously. "You can use me because I can do something new!"

He clasped his hands behind his back and stared at me, looking me over from head to toe and back again. "Well?" I asked.

"What is the something new you speak of?"

"It's a play called *Hototogisu*."

"The Cuckoo?" He smiled.

"The Nightingale," I corrected him. "It's by Tokutomi Roka. Why don't you do it? I will play the hero Takeo, the young naval lieutenant."

"I don't doubt you certainly would like to," Fujita remarked. "Just what experience have you had at acting?"

"None."

"None! You have never put so much as one foot on a stage or spoken a line, and yet you march back here, call me out, damn the play, damn my management policy and proceed to tell me that you can do better!"

"I am confident I can," I said.

"What's the play about?" he asked, snapping at me.

I proceeded to explain the plot scene by scene, taking

the roles of Takeo and Namiko, the girl, by turns. It had little trouble remembering, for the story was all but engraved on my brain. I had read it as a novel when I was in school. One of my friends in Nanaura was the son of a priest. I went to visit him at his home one afternoon and found him hunched up in one corner of his room, reading a book and crying as if his heart would break. I naturally asked him why.

"I can't help it, Kintaro," he sniffed. He waved the book at me. "It's this book."

I looked and saw that the title was *Hototogisu.* "What's it about?"

"It's a sad story about a man who has to leave his sick wife. You should read it."

"And you shouldn't," I said, suddenly feeling terribly self-righteous. "You, the son of a priest. You shouldn't be reading this sort of romantic nonsense. You should be studying."

Curiosity, however, soon got the better of me. I took the book from him and began to page through it. Irresistibly drawn in, I read some thirty pages before my friend interrupted to exchange tit for tat, and remarked that as the son of the governor I shouldn't be reading it either.

"Lend it to me," I begged.

What I had read demanded I read more. I took the book home, and because I would be scolded if my father or mother discovered me reading it, I made a plain paper cover for it. On the outside of the cover I wrote, "Lectures in Algebra," and sat down to continue my reading. The story tore at my heart as much as it had that of my friend. I began to cry, and was gushing great sentimental tears when my cousin, a girl some three years older than I, found me.

She looked at the name I had written on the cover. "If algebra is that difficult, perhaps I should help you."

I quickly put the book aside and blew my nose. Somehow

I changed the subject and got her to leave. Then I went
back to reading. I read the story again and again until I
knew every character and could practically recount their
dialogue verbatim. Later, when the novel was made into
a play, I went to Tokyo to see it, and cried some more.

Fujita was near tears himself when I finished telling
him the story. "It's good," he conceded, "very good. Perhaps
you do have something to offer."

"Then you'll let me play it?" I asked anxiously.

He looked at me in silence. "Yes," he said finally. "Yes,
I will. Come into my office. I want you to tell me more
about yourself."

We passed the rest of the night in conversation. It was
nearly morning when I got back to my hotel. When the
office of the steamship line opened, I canceled my ticket
and went back to Little Tokyo to locate a copy of *Hototogisu*. The one thing I neglected to tell Toyo Fujita was
that I didn't have a copy of the novel, much less a script
of the play!

6   The Boat Before the Wind

THE JAPANESE THEATRE WAS NOT A FULL-TIME OPERATION.
The playhouse was permanent, but most of the actors and
actresses who worked for Toyo Fujita had other jobs.
Plays were produced on the average of once a month, and
ran about four days to a week each. The situation was
indicative of amateurs, but the quality of the acting was
professional. The girl who played opposite me in *Hototogisu* had been a geisha in Tokyo, and from her previous
experience was able to give an almost flawless performance
of Namiko.

My production of Tokutomi Roka's tearfully romantic
story received very good reviews from the critic of the
Japanese newspaper in Los Angeles, and those of the other
papers.

I must confess that Fujita produced the play with mis-
giving. He said he admired my confidence, but worried

about my ability. But the role of Takeo the young Japanese naval lieutenant was one of second nature to me. My training at the Naval Preparatory School in Tokyo gave me all the insight into how Takeo should conduct himself; my feeling and understanding for the story supplied the necessary emotion.

It remained for me, not being familiar with any method of acting or style of stage conduct, to let my portrayal flow naturally from me. The power of concentration developed by Zen practice enabled me to expel the consciousness of what little technique I may have thought about and subdue any desire to exercise my ego. Rather, I entered into a state of identity and oneness with the part. The exact awareness of playing the part was done away with. The result was that I gave a very realistic performance.

When one is highly conscious of what one is doing, the result is apt to be less than what is really possible to achieve. Once, shortly before a performance, someone made a point of telling me a very important person was sitting in the audience. My thought was that I must act well and impress that person. Consequently, I went on stage and did not act well for some ten minutes. But then I understood what had happened to me. I was working hard at trying to impress someone, and the conscious evil of the attempt was hurting my performance. The interference of nongenuine and ulterior intentions is the reason "show-offs" never succeed.

After the final curtain came down on the first performance of *Hototogisu,* Fujita visited me in the dressing room. He shook his head in wonder. "I have the feeling I should salute," he laughed. "I'm sure a good bit of the audience feels the same way."

"Do you think I should continue?"

"Frankly, I don't think it is for me to say. I actually didn't think you would do as well as you have," he admitted. "I thought this sort of thing—a total stranger bursting in on the producer and selling himself—only happens in stories and plays. You amaze me, you really do.

"You mentioned something about going home—returning to Japan. Do you still plan to do so?" he asked.

"One success doesn't prove much," I said. "I will stay."

"Good. Think about the next play."

He left and went to his office to count the receipts. I finished removing my makeup and got into my street clothes. When I left the theatre to take a walk and get something to eat before going to bed, a group of people from the audience were still standing out in front of the theatre talking. They were discussing the play—and me! And favorably. It made me feel very good.

I followed my performance in *Hototogisu* with appearances in a number of Japanese plays, some old, some new. My name began to stand for good entertainment and I was pointed out on the street and in the restaurants.

Toward the close of summer, when Little Tokyo celebrated Japan Day, and became gay and happy from end to end, I talked my way into participating in the judo and *kendo* exhibitions that were part of the festivities. I won both my matches. That evening, I ran into the man I bested and his girl friend in a restaurant. The girl, in a sudden display of admiration, came over to me and kissed the large bruise I had on my right arm from the *kendo* match. The man nearly exploded with anger. "Fop," he called me, and asked, "What is your name?"

"Hayakawa," I replied, rising to my feet and shifting into the judo starting position. "I'm ready any time you are ready."

We stood glaring at each other. The girl looked from my face to his and waited, frightened that a fight would start and thrilled that it might. Finally, the man backed off, grabbed her arm and walked away.

The gossips spread accounts of this incident throughout

the Japanese community, and my name became better known than ever. The name of Kintaro, however, I thought about dropping. It didn't ring as I imagined an actor's name should. I considered changing it for a long time before deciding to call myself Hokushu. The great general Saigo Nanshu, whom I admired, was responsible for this idea. Because Nanshu means south in Japanese, I wanted to call myself Hokushu, which means north.

"But there is already someone by that name here," Toyo Fujita told me when I informed him of my choice. "You'll have to choose something else."

I compromised. Since there was snow in the north, I decided to call myself Setsu, which, when pronounced as Sesshu or Sessue, means snow. So, I became Sessue Hayakawa.

Acting at the Japanese Theatre was not enough to make my living, so when the play season was over I went back to working as an iceman. I got a job at an ice plant on Catalina Island off the California coast near Los Angeles. It was hard work—pure backbreaking labor—but I refused to let myself be beaten by it. I carried four cakes to everyone else's one. The example of stamina reflected in my pay check. I received more wages than the other ice luggers, and in two months was able to save a fair amount to be put by against the expenses of the coming fall and winter. Then the theatre season would begin again and I could return to acting.

"Now what? I know that look." I had returned to work at the Japanese Theatre and was bearding Toyo Fujita in his office. "Out with it. What have you in mind now?" he pressed.

Being a success only among the Japanese had come to dissatisfy me. I wanted to be better known outside Little Tokyo. If I am going to act in America, I should act for Americans, I thought.

"I find our Japanese plays and Japanese audiences confining," I told Fujita. "I want an English-speaking audience to see and hear what I have to offer. I want to act for Americans. And in something they can understand, something that will reach them. A Japanese play won't do, even in translation."

"You are ambitious, aren't you?"

"Why not?"

"It will have to be something with popular appeal, of course," Fujita observed. "Have you a play in mind? Can you do it? And, most of all, do you think they'll accept you?"

"They will in the right play."

I was already thinking of the right play. During my last weeks at college I had gone again and again to see a play called *Typhoon*. Most of the characters in it were Japanese. They had been played by Americans—Occidentals in Oriental guise—whose stage voices reflected little of the Japanese nuance and inflection when speaking English— save artificial mispronunciation and poor grammar— neither of which was authentic. For all of this, though, the play had captivated me with its sheer dramatic appeal.

A political melodrama with its action motivated by a stark touch of romantic tragedy, *Typhoon* was, I explained to Fujita, originally written by a Hungarian playwright named Melchior Lengyel. Adapted into English by Laurence Irving, the youngest son of the first English actor ever to be knighted, Sir Henry Irving, and a noted actor-producer in his own right, *Typhoon* enjoyed a run of more than two hundred performances at four theatres in London in the spring of 1913.

In the play, Laurence Irving performed the role of Tokoramo, who is both hero and villain in the piece. The British critics gave him excellent reviews, and pointed out that to them he seemed more Japanese than the real Japanese he employed in his cast. Among the actors who

supported Irving in the play was a young man named
Claude Rains.

Typhoon was produced and sent on tour in the United
States with Walker Whiteside in the role created by Laurence Irving. Whiteside was the actor I had seen and
admired in the play over and over again from my cheap
balcony seat in Chicago. His role—Irving's—was the one
I proposed performing for my first American audience.

The title of the play, *Typhoon*, is a deceiving one. The
play is not, as one might suspect, a South Seas saga replete
with naïve Polynesians, lusting white traders, a fabulous
treasure of rare egg-sized pearls guarded in a sacred lagoon
by a giant squid, and a violent tropical storm which sweeps
in at the climax to punish the evildoers and unite the lovers
as the final curtain descends.

"The title is symbolic of the conflict of human emotions
under tremendous stress," I told Fujita. "Like most of
life which is dignified and noble, the plot is simple. An
educated man, a man of letters, Tokoramo is a ranking
member of a diplomatic mission residing in the Japanese
colony in Paris. He is an important figure there, and vital
to the success of what his group is carrying on. He has a
lover, a French girl, with whom he tries to break off. He
accuses her of unfaithfulness and they argue and he
strangles her."

"And? Go on, go on." Excited, Fujita got up and began
to pace back and forth in front of his desk.

"He confides what he has done to the other members of
the mission. It is decided he is too important to be given
over to the police to stand trial and go to prison. Out of
patriotic zeal, a young member of the group, Hironari,
offers to confess. He does so, but at his trial Tokoramo is
overcome with remorse and breaks into the proceedings to
tell the truth. But no one believes him. Instead, the
authorities think his confession is an attempt to save

Hironari. Because of it, the innocent young man willing to sacrifice himself is thought all the more guilty. He is sentenced to death.

"Tokoramo is free to go on with his work, but his guilt gnaws at him. The *bushido* spirit won't let him rest. Finally, he confesses to the man he thinks was his rival in love, only to learn this man refused the dead girl's favors because he knew how much Tokoramo cared for her. He forgives the Japanese, who then feels a great weight has been lifted from his shoulders."

At this point in my explanation of the play I got carried away. In my mind's eye, I could see Walker Whiteside as Tokoramo. I recalled his movements, the way he walked, and began to act out part of the drama.

"Listen to this!" I exclaimed. "Tokoramo is thanking his mistaken rival for understanding his crime of passion. 'Stretching your hand to me out in forgiveness, many steps have you climbed, and many steps have you raised me, towards that goal—nirvana, as we call it—that goal of perfect calm which draws us back at last, after thousands of earthly existences have been cast aside, back to the perfect essence of our being.' "

"Tremendous!" Fujita crowed. Having seated himself while I spoke as Tokoramo, he bounded to his feet and clasped me by the hands. "Wonderful! And you think an American audience will accept a Japanese company in this play?"

"I'm sure of it," I said. "To begin with, the play is in English. Oh, it is an adaptation into English, but what I mean is it is not just something done into English from Japanese solely to attract an English-speaking audience. It has all the dramatic values an American theatre goer loves. Whiteside was a great hit in it."

"He was with you, Sessue, no doubt about that. You

probably know the play by heart the same way you know
the play you talked me into producing with you."

I grinned and nodded. "Almost by heart," I said.

"Do the play. By all means, do it." Fujita urged me
as I turned to leave his office. "By the way," he asked as
my hand gripped the knob of the door leading backstage,
"how does *Typhoon* end?"

"Tokoramo commits hara-kiri," I said, my stomach
muscles suddenly contracting. I left and let other thoughts
occupy my mind.

"Opportunity knocks but once," is the core of a well-
known proverb in the Western world. I think that everyone, at least once in life, is given an opportunity which, if
recognized and grasped, leads on to one or another form of
success—personal or public, professional or private, spiritual or material. When opportunity knocks, whether you
make the best of it or let it pass is the decisive factor for
success or failure.

It is a mistake to believe that opportunity is easy to come
by. More often opportunity is made rather than found;
when it knocks it has been invited, not waited for. One
must be prepared to take advantage of opportunity.

People often say of a person, "He is lucky" or "He has
good luck." Success is not a matter of luck. Everyone is
given a fortune. Whether a man has a good fortune or a
bad one depends upon how it is used. But it seldom
happens that one has a good life or a bad life as a mere
result of having a good fortune or a bad fortune.

Success, I think, lies in oneself. Opportunity must be
made as often as it is found or placed in one's way.

The Japanese mostly think that a good successful life is
an accidental event; that such a thing is given to someone

by someone else. There is a possibility that everybody can get such a gift. But most of the time, people let it pass by.

I believe that self-confidence backed by sound knowledge of what you want to do and disciplined by solid spiritual principle is the secret of success. One need not live by his wits nor wait for opportunity if he has self-confidence, sound ambition, and a will to work hard.

Zen is a religion of action. It does not move in ruts. It demands that one act—move with life. It preaches "self-power," and thus gives lie to the belief that all things come to him who waits.

What mastery of self I achieved through Zen practice provided me with the determination to succeed in my ambition to play for and satisfy an American audience. Fujita did not know it, but I had meditated a long time before concluding to go ahead with my plan to produce *Typhoon.* I rarely make snap judgments or quick decisions. All of consequence that I have undertaken during my career and in my private life has been carefully considered. For what I do produces karma. And while I am lastly in the hands of destiny, I, as well as any man, can choose what deeds are to be done. Once done, however, they cannot be undone. The results must be accepted; I am subject to them. Therefore, it is imperative I move the pieces on my chessboard of human existence in such way as to not hinder my journey to nirvana.

This is not merely a matter of doing the right thing, but of believing as you act.

I had confidence, ambition and a will to strive for success. But I had no money, no dramatic company and no theatre. Only a play.

If ever anyone started on a shoestring, I did. I went to the Eagan Dramatic School in Los Angeles for actors. To my delight, eight people responded. Among them were Henry Kotani and Thomas Kurihara, both of whom I later worked with in motion pictures. My offer was simple: "I want to produce the play of *Typhoon* with Japanese actors for an American audience. I can't promise you salaries, only some payment if we are successful. Will you do it?"

They would, and they did. Everyone I assembled for the cast caught my enthusiasm and pitched in bent on succeeding. I then traded on my success at the Japanese Theatre. I raised some money from some of the owners of the restaurants I had patronized in Little Tokyo; and talked the Japanese carpenters in the section into building our settings on credit. With some of the funds I raised I rented the Elks Lodge hall on Spring Street, in what is now the heart of Los Angeles. The rest of the cast and I rehearsed for a month.

Laurence Irving opened his production of *Typhoon* at London's Haymarket Theatre on April 2, 1913. I opened mine approximately one year later. The play brought considerable success to Irving when he did it. I hoped it would do as much for me and my company. In all, there were twenty-one in the cast—nineteen men and two women. I had been able to recruit practically every Japanese actor in Los Angeles. I had begged and borrowed lights and talked the electricians into running them without pay. Now it was up to the public.

We were a novelty—I'm sure many who came to see us thought that—but we drew good houses from the start. Word got around. Curiosity and love of the theatre put a line at the box office. I achieved my goal! The production satisfied our American audiences.

After the curtain had come down on the fourth and final act the third night we were performing, a short, somewhat cherubic-looking man, dressed in what I guessed was yacht- ing dress—a dark and loosely tied bow flopping above an expanse of white shirt—came into my dressing room and introduced himself as, "Thomas Ince, Mr. Hayakawa. I'll talk while you get cleaned up."

I had never heard of him, but I listened.

"I make motion pictures," he said, "and I want to film your production of *Typhoon* as a picture. With you playing the part you play now, of course."

Frankly, the idea did not appeal to me. Nowadays, the opportunity is snapped up without a second thought. But in 1914 motion pictures were only a few years old. They were growing, and they were successful, but they were still speculative. I thought the idea over as I removed my make-up.

Mr. Ince continued to talk. "Right now, I'm making western thrillers—cowboys and horses, all that, in Santa Monica. If you'd like to come out to the studio, I'd . . ."

"No," I said, breaking in. "I don't think so."

"Good lord, man, why not? The play's terrific for a picture. It has stature, a message—everything. The public will go wild over it."

I still hesitated. It's funny to think of it now, but, frankly, the thought of traveling to Santa Monica day after day while the picture was shooting dampened my interest.

But Mr. Ince was not to be put off. "*Typhoon* is just the thing for what we call a feature," he explained. "It's different, and won't be only entertainment."

"I'd like it to be something more than a thriller." I was weakening. The more he talked, the more I became interested. "What can you pay a week?"

He named an amount which far exceeded the sum I felt I was lucky enough to save out of my earnings lugging ice in Catalina.

"That much?"

"I want to do the picture," Mr. Ince said with emphasis.

"The company—the others," I asked, "will you use them?"

"I'll use everybody in some way. But I would prefer to replace your main supporting actor and the heroine with people of my own."

"I must think about it," I said.

"Thin—ahhh." He let his breath out slowly and smiled. "All right, think about it. I'll be in touch with you." We shook hands and he moved toward the door. "You Orientals," he said as he went out, "you're all as cautious as cats!"

Thomas H. Ince, when I first met him that night, had only ten years to live. He was to die under mysterious circumstances in 1924. One of the greatest directors of the silent screen era, he was one of the most thorough film-makers of his or any time. Hollywood today owes him a debt for developing what is known as a shooting script.

In the early days motion pictures were many times made on a catch-as-catch-can basis. Mack Sennett, whose Keystone Comedies delighted and regaled millions for close to twenty years before sound films were perfected, recalled following the Los Angeles Fire Department on a call, setting up his camera and instructing his funnymen to improvise on the spot while the flames roared. Even the legendary D. W. Griffith, the maker of *Birth of a Nation* and *Intolerance*, although he used a sort of script, used to debate what was to be done, change it and change again as the picture progressed.

But Ince was a perfectionist who preferred to have his ideas and inspirations beforehand, put them carefully on paper and work from them in an organized and orderly manner.

He had left a career as a stage actor to work in motion pictures beginning in 1910, in New York, where the

industry started. Within two years he was in Hollywood
heading a division of the New York Motion Picture
Company, and making westerns on a scale which pointed
the way to the big feature films of today.

Ince liked lots of everything—actors, action and scenery—
in his pictures. Part of his studio in Santa Monica housed
a complete Wild West troupe, the famous Miller Brothers'
101 Ranch Show.

A tireless organizer and worker who knew every phase
of the business well, Ince outgrew westerns within a few
years; when he suddenly appeared before me with his offer,
he was determined to take another big step forward.

When Ince called on me he was heading his own
company as an independent producer-director. He released
his pictures himself or sold them to distributors. He told
me *Typhoon* would blaze a new trail.

Ince had a great deal of vision and enthusiasm, both of
which rubbed off on me. We talked a second time and a
third, however, before I agreed to his proposition.

"But these are the conditions," I told him. "Hire all
those working with me, give us a three-month contract and
transportation to and from the studio. Santa Monica's a
long way to go to work every day."

He agreed to my terms. Production on the film began
as soon as the play closed its run at the Elks Hall. Mr. Ince
supervised but did not direct. He assigned that task to a
man named Reginald Barker. I, of course, played the role
of Tokoramo. The other major characters were portrayed
by Henry Kotani, Thomas Kurihara, Gladys Brockwell,
Leona Hutton and Frank Borzage. Both Kotani and Kurihara were countrymen of mine. Between 1914 and 1920
they were leaders among the small band of Japanese actors
who contributed to the growth of American films. After
the First World War, when Japanese film-makers decided
to modernize and follow the lead of Hollywood, they were

called back to Japan. They both became directors, and as
such introduced American techniques.

Another member of the *Typhoon* cast who became a
director was Frank Borzage, with whom I became good
friends during the time we worked for Ince. I found Frank
a good-hearted, congenial companion. As inquisitive of
life as I was, he was a man with whom I could talk seriously. He was not an educated man. Frank never got
beyond grammar school. But he possessed a high degree of
native intelligence and an ability to learn. From the very
first, I saw he was an observer. He did not remain an actor
for very long. Frank had the spark and drive which
appealed to Ince, who made him a director and taught
him all he could. Frank learned and developed quickly.
He went on to direct Charles Farrell and Janet Gaynor
in *Seventh Heaven* and Gary Cooper and Helen Hayes in
the first film version of Ernest Hemingway's novel, *A
Farwell To Arms* For his direction of *Seventh Heaven*
he received an Academy Award in 1928, the first year the
presentations were made. Ince would have been very
proud of Frank.

The first time I saw the Thomas H. Ince Productions
studio in Santa Monica—Inceville, it was called—it looked
to me like one great Texas ranch. Cowboys, a small tribe
of Sioux Indians, horses and cattle, filled it. The stages for
shooting scenes consisted of canvas stretched on wooden
frames for walls, with cheesecloth ceilings which could be
pulled over to reduce the sunlight when night scenes were
taken. Not having to worry about sound, you acted amid a
babble of voices and a roar of activity. In spite of Mr.
Ince's organization, the work went on noisily and in what
impressed the outsider as an atmosphere of utter confusion.
When I wasn't in front of the camera or discussing a coming
scene with Mr. Barker, I found relief in sitting and medi-

tating. I went off by myself to some reasonably quiet corner, concentrated and shut out all distraction. The practice, if only for a few minutes, was a great restorative. I can today read a book in Times Square at the height of the New York rush hour as if I were the only one in the world and alone in the middle of a desert.

We had worked on *Typhoon* two or three days when Mr. Ince and Mr. Barker showed me a can of film they called "the rushes," the first reel of scenes taken. They invited me to see it with them.

"It's going to be great," Mr. Ince said as we filed into the darkness of his projection room.

"I shot it just the way you wanted," Mr. Barker told him. I learned this was true to the letter. Ince made a practice of laying out his picture plans in such detail that he could, and would, stamp "Produce this exactly as written!" on the script, and it would be done.

"Is that me?" My voice broke in embarrassment as the film unreeled and I saw myself on the screen for the first time. I turned to Mr. Ince in shame. "Terrible, it's terrible!" I stood up. "I'm not going to do it!"

"Sessue! My god!" he exclaimed.

"It's not me, it's—some idiot!" I felt quite pale and walked outside. Mr. Ince and Reginald Barker followed me.

I went over to a chair and sat down, putting my head in my hands. "I'm sorry, Mr. Ince. I'm going back to Los Angeles."

"Ridiculous," he said. "But, if you insist, I'll drive you back."

We walked to his car, a large open car with brass headlights. I got in and sat in silence while he started it and drove away from Inceville toward Los Angeles. "Everybody feels that way when they see themselves for the first time," he said as we bumped over the road winding through the Santa Monica mountains. "Not only you."

From the time we left the studio until we reached Los Angeles where he took me to a restaurant for dinner and drinks, Mr. Ince cajoled, lectured, pleaded, did everything to cure my disappointment.

For some reason, as I sat listening to him, a *koan* popped into my head. "Unless, at one time, perspiration has streamed down your back, you cannot see the boat sailing before the wind." I drifted into thought as to whether I had been rash in my reaction and entertained some false conception of vanity. I had been quite unprepared for the shock of seeing myself flickering on the screen. It gives one a strange sensation the first time.

"Well?" Mr. Ince's voice suddenly cut into my reverie.

I fished in my mind for some answer. "I will have to think it over," I said lamely. I finished my drink and put down the glass.

"You will not!" he exploded good-naturedly. He laughed. "The last time you thought it over, Sessue, I almost lost what I think is a very good thing."

I hesitated, then gave in. "All right, I'll go back."

Shooting on *Typhoon* resumed the next day, and nothing more was said about my cold feet.

Let me go back a bit.

The year 1914 was one of many turning points in my life. Seven years before I had been bent upon a naval career, deprived of this ambition; and the year following I had tried to commit suicide. Now I found myself on the verge of attaining greater heights than I ever dreamed of. Mr. Ince painted a bright and successful future for me as a motion picture actor; but a greater part of my future involved being a husband.

When I went to the Eagan Dramatic School to recruit actors for my stage production of *Typhoon*, I was introduced to a young Japanese girl named Tsuru Aoki.

"I was born in Japan, but I have been here since I was six," she said in answer to my immediate curiosity. "And I am twenty. Why?"

She looked at me out of dark luminous eyes set in a bewitching face, and inclined her head slightly while a tender smile commented on what she saw.

I suddenly felt flustered and out of my element. I excused myself and left her to interview some other students.

Tsuru Aoki, however, engaged my thoughts a great deal from then on. I learned that she was the niece of the Kawakamis, an internationally famous Japanese husband and wife acting team. They brought her to the United States as a member of their touring company. But in San Francisco, the first stop on the tour, the authorities had forbidden Tsuru to appear, ruling that she was too young. Informed this would happen practically everywhere they went in the United States, the Kawakamis left Tsuru with a San Francisco friend, the noted Japanese artist Hyosai Aoki, who placed her in a Catholic convent. As the years passed, Tsuru came to look upon Aoki as her father, her natural parents both being dead, and took his name. He died while she was at the convent, and an American newspaper woman adopted Tsuru and brought her to live in Los Angeles, where she grew to girlhood and began studying to become an actress.

She fascinated me. But I did not engage her for *Typhoon*. Instead, I paid her court. She accepted my invitations to dinner and came to see me in the play.

Tsuru was a rare person to find in Los Angeles in 1914. I had never met anyone like her; I have not met anyone like her since. Her character is as I have always found it to be, sincere and tender. I met her and thought back to the formality which marked my early training, and in her saw the qualities of nobleness, charity and courage.

I wasn't the only one interested in her. The romance which blossomed between us touched off considerable jealousy. A number of other young Japanese men coveted her companionship, and I was hard-pressed to win out. One of my rivals went so far as to challenge me to a duel for her hand.

Until I met Tsuru Aoki, I had not given much thought to marrying, except to make a mental note not to marry a girl who was taller than I was. I had not paid much attention to girls while at college. I don't recall that there were any Japanese girls at the university when I was there, and the American girls interested me very little. They were too forward and independent.

But in Los Angeles, while I acted at the Japanese Theatre, things changed and I changed. Suddenly I was twenty-four years old, engaged in a career and eligible. And just as suddenly, I met Tsuru Aoki and my eligibility became vital to me.

Late April, 1914, found us in the middle of making *Typhoon* in Inceville. I spent the days in front of the camera, twilights driving into Los Angeles in the chauffeur-driven Packard landaulet Mr. Ince provided for my use, nights at dinner with Tsuru. I was over my uneasiness at seeing myself on film and was going about the work with intense professional concentration.

Almost from the moment I met her I had thoughts of marrying Tsuru. But I had promised myself not to marry until I had saved a thousand dollars.

Saving it, however, was not the problem it would have been the evening I opened *Typhoon* at the Elks Hall,

wondering where the money to pay my debts would come
from if the play failed. Mr. Ince was paying me more per
week than I had been able to earn during all the summers
I carried ice while at college in Chicago! It amazed me. In
those early Hollywood days, it was busboy one day, high-
paid comedian or romantic lead the next. From 1912, when
the motion picture industry first spread its wings in Hollywood, until the great stock market crash of 1929, salaries
spiraled upward almost beyond belief. Two years after I
made *Typhoon* I was earning $7,500 a week. After World
War I, stars like William S. Hart, Geraldine Farrar and
Alla Nazimova were paid $10,000 and more per week.

I had the money, and I asked Tsuru to marry me one
evening when we were out rowing in East Lake Park, in
Los Angeles. She accepted, and said she had been waiting
for me to ask her. We were married in a Japanese ceremony
in Little Tokyo's Zen temple on May 1, 1914.

Mr. Ince gave me four days off from the studio to go on
my honeymoon. Tsuru and I drove to San Diego and the
resort town near it, La Jolla. I purchased an automobile for the trip, a Case; and drove for the first time in my
life after receiving a few instructions from the previous
owner.

"Put it in first gear to start, then in second, then in high,"
he explained. "Go into first going uphill and downhill."
I understood how to start it, feed the gas, brake and steer,
but I couldn't shift gears very well.

We gritted our teeth all the way to La Jolla, but we
arrived safely and thoroughly enjoyed ourselves. But
coming back, I left the car in neutral while going down a
steep hill, rode the pedal and burned out the brakes. The
Case rolled to a stop, and from then on we crept north
until we reached a small town south of Los Angeles and a
tire blew out. We left the car and I took Tsuru to a hotel

and saw that the car was brought to a nearby garage. "In the morning, everything will be fixed," I said.

Tsuru just looked at me. She stared until I realized we had spent the last of our money for gasoline before leaving San Diego.

"I have this watch and there's her watch and ring," I told the hotel manager when we came down from our room to check out. "I can send you what we owe tomorrow. I'm starring in a motion picture, *Typhoon*, and . . ."

The manager looked at me and shook his head. "Never heard of it."

"I'm starring."

He shrugged, but smiled. "On your honeymoon?"

I nodded, embarrassed. Tsuru laughed softly and turned to look out the front window of the hotel lobby.

The hotel manager drummed his fingers on the registry desk and pursed his lips in thought. Then he grinned. "Young man, since you're on your honeymoon this is on me." He marked our hotel bill paid and walked with us to the garage and paid the mechanic.

The following morning when I reported on the set in Inceville to continue work on *Typhoon*, I sent a man to the hotel to repay the manager whose genuine kindness had melted an awkward and embarrassing situation.

Then I got ready for the first scene of the day, and promptly broke out laughing. I roared at nothing in particular. I felt extremely happy and exhilarated. And my feeling was the only excuse I could give for my state. No matter how hard I tried to control myself and concentrate on my work, I giggled and laughed. I finally got so bad we had to stop shooting altogether.

"I thought you Japanese kept your emotions buried somewhere," Reginald Barker fumed at me.

I could do nothing but shake my head and laugh. I tried to concentrate on something and pull myself together, but no sooner would I get my face composed than the urge to laugh burst to the surface anew and I was off again. Mr. Barker ran his hands through his hair in exasperation, lighted a cigarette and wandered off in the direction of Mr. Ince's office. I left the set and walked around the studio trying to get a grip on myself while the rest of the cast and crew lounged and drank coffee.

Typhoon was made while a major change in the business end of the motion picture industry was taking place. The Paramount Pictures Corporation was being organized by a well-known exhibitor named W. W. Hodkinson, who, to facilitate distribution, brought together Adolph Zukor and his Famous Players in Famous Plays Company, The Jesse Lasky Feature Play Company, Pallas Pictures, Morosco Pictures, and a number of the smaller studios. The most important of the contributing film companies were the Famous Players which Adolph Zukor founded with Daniel Frohman, the New York stage producer; and the Lasky company which consisted of Mr. Lasky, the company's director-general Cecil B. De Mille, and Samuel Goldwyn, whose name then was Goldfish. The Lasky company, too, had a close association with the theatre in New York. A supporter of it was David Belasco.

In addition to drawing upon the companies which signed contracts for distribution with it, the Paramount Pictures Corporation purchased films from independent producers such as Thomas H. Ince. Mr. Ince sold *Typhoon* to Paramount which booked it to open and play at the first real theatre in the United States exclusively devoted to motion pictures, the Strand on Broadway between Forty-seventh and Forty-eighth streets in New York City.

Immediately after completing *Typhoon* and selling it to

Paramount at a considerable profit, Mr. Ince started me making another picture, *The Wrath of the Gods.* This was a spectacular production, and it pointed the way toward the epic films D. W. Griffith and Cecil B. De Mille undertook to produce within a few years.

The Wrath of the Gods was the second picture I made for Mr. Ince. Shortly after it was completed my contract expired and I received an offer from the Lasky company.

"Well, I've got an offer of my own to make," Mr. Ince said when he heard another studio was interested in having my services. "Stay with me two or three more years, Sessue. I'll do the best I can, and give you a hundred-dollar-a-week raise every six months."

I reserved making my decision and talked again with the Lasky company representative. "How much is your biggest star getting?" I asked.

"One thousand dollars a week."

I thought Mr. Ince paid me well, but not this well. I tried not to seem too impressed. "If you think I'm worth it, I wouldn't want any more than that," I said. "Will you pay me a thousand dollars a week?"

One thousand dollars a week to start, and an increase of five hundred dollars every six months was the offer the Lasky company was willing to make me. I told Mr. Ince.

The words no sooner left my mouth than he was out of his chair. He smashed out his cigar and shook his head. "It's a lie," he said.

"I don't lie, Mr. Ince."

"Well, I don't mean that—but a thousand a week on the strength of a couple of pictures. I certainly can't go it."

"Then I'm going to sign with them," I said.

He didn't believe me. That he didn't showed in his eyes. But he didn't make me another offer. We stood looking at each other in silence for a while. Then he said, "O.K., Sessue, sign with 'em," and waved me away.

I left Inceville and drove into Hollywood and signed a contract with the Lasky company. A few days later, Mr. Ince got in touch with me and asked me to sign a contract with him again. "You told me to sign with Lasky, so I did," I reminded him. He was dumbfounded. He refused to believe I really had signed until I showed him my contract.

"Well, it serves me right," he commented. "Damn!"

I saw very little of Mr. Ince after I went to work for the Lasky company, but his name and his accomplishments in pictures were always mentioned when people got to talking about the creative end of the business. By 1916, he was heading a five-hundred-thousand-dollar studio in Culver City, where Universal Pictures was established. Then he was a partner with D. W. Griffith and Mack Sennett in the Triangle Company. But after that venture collapsed in 1917 he slowly declined in influence and brilliance. He made pictures right up until his sudden death in 1924, but none had the spark that made his first films major contributions.

Among the arts practiced in Japan which both mystify and intrigue those of the Western world is the art of physiognomy. *Ninso* it is called. It has been prevalent in Japan for centuries.

A *ninso* practitioner can judge a person by facial appearance and expression. He can tell what a person has done or has not done, and what or what not is planned. Also, he can, to an extent, foretell the future.

People laugh at a professing of belief in what the *ninso* expert says, but I think there are those among us who can tell, partially if not completely and accurately, what kind of person you are and whether you will succeed or fail in the future. I have very good reason to believe this way: the predictions of strangers have more than twice come true for me. And they have, in spite of my own beliefs and actions which ran counter to them.

For instance, I did not move quickly to accept the opportunity Mr. Ince offered when he called on me in my dressing room at the Elks Hall in Los Angeles following the third performance of my production of *Typhoon*. I was reluctant to consider his proposition at first, and had to be convinced. I was not even remotely interested in becoming a motion picture actor when he asked me to do the film of the play. I had undertaken to stage *Typhoon* mainly because I was dissatisfied by the narrowness of performing only for Japanese audiences. I had felt confined—limited by the restriction put on my performing as an actor by the special appeal of the Japanese theatre. I considered myself somewhat in the position of Eugene O'Neill's actor-father when the public made it clear it wasn't particularly interested in seeing James O'Neill in anything else but the play of *The Count of Monte Cristo*.

I wanted to do different and better things. I was interested in proving the scope of what I believed I had to offer the general public—American audiences as well as Japanese. What happened thereafter shows the influence one life may have upon the course of another. A total stranger appears on your doorstep and your destiny changes. I believe therefore, although I may choose what deeds I do, the karma of others affects my destiny as well. But for Mr. Ince I would have returned to Japan and a destiny in harmony with the conditions under which my father allowed me to come to the United States.

The law of causality is strange in its working. The more I consider cause and effect, the more it seems to me I am manipulated like a marionette by the strings of destiny.

And one's destiny is shaped by many causes. I scoffed at the prediction of the melon vendor in Little Tokyo. What could he have read in my face, I thought later, to indicate my future? The developments of the future proved his prediction true, of course, but when he made it my mind was too inhibited to accept it seriously. I treated his prediction the same way I responded to the predictions of the old man my sister and I visited near Nanaura. Parts of his claimed foreknowledge of my future had come to pass; and because they had, I should have paused to consider the words of the melon vendor in a reasonable light. But his moment, like that of the other fortuneteller, failed to impress me until I reached a point in life from where I could look back and see their wisdom.

And so it seems things always appear clearer in retrospect. We can better judge then. And when we judge what we might have become and what we might have done, all that we intended and anticipated takes on less value, and the outcome of our lives appears a natural end to whatever has happened.

But so much is predestined. And, being predestined, will occur.

Myself as a naval cadet
at the age of fifteen.

In an early starring role.

In *The Cheat,* 1915.

In *Son of Heaven,* a Cecil B. De Mille picture.

My Hollywood castle at the corner of Franklin Street
and Argyle Avenue.

My wife Tsuru and I in 1931.

Tsuru with our son Yukio and our daughter Aoki.

Welcomed home to Tokyo in 1932.

At a cocktail party in Paris I gave to celebrate my return to the screen in 1937. At my right is Mlle. Tanaka, the Japanese opera star. The other guests are Parisiennes in Japanese costume.

Jack Iwata

The opening of an exhibition of my paintings
in Los Angeles, 1949.

Cecil B. De Mille shows me a model property and a set design
for his epic motion picture, *The Ten Commandments*.

With Claudette Colbert in *Three Came Home*, 1949.

As Colonel Saito in *The Bridge on the River Kwai*, 1958.

United Press

I receive the Golden Globe Award, Hollywood, 1958.

Myself as I look today.

7   Seeds are being Planted

I WENT TO WORK FOR THE LASKY COMPANY LESS THAN A
year after entering motion pictures with Thomas H. Ince.
My sudden jump in salary was no more startling when I
changed studios than it had been when I was signed to
make *Typhoon*. The studios wanted and needed interesting people with talent whom they could build up in the
public mind, and they were willing to pay in proportion
to public response. My performances in *Typhoon* and
The Wrath of the Gods had prompted a show of public
interest. The Lasky company wanted to foster it further,
and quite willingly agreed to pay me what I said I would
like to have.

When I joined it, the Jesse Lasky Feature Play Company
had its studio at 6284 Selma Avenue, in Hollywood. This
was the corner of Selma and Vine Street, which, until films

began to be made there, was a cow pasture. In fact, a major portion of the studio was a barn. Cecil B. De Mille's first film, *The Squaw Man*, which starred Dustin Farnum and is often referred to as the first real feature film, was photographed in the barn. The barn still stands, carefully preserved, within the walls of the Paramount Studios of today. It is California Registered Landmark No. 554, "Hollywood's First Major Film Company Studio."

Although I reported to the studio immediately after leaving Mr. Ince, it was some months before I got in front of the camera. The Lasky company had wanted me, had hired me but couldn't use me. Not right away.

Finally, late in 1915, I was cast in *The Cheat*, a film since singled out by one motion picture historian, Lewis Jacobs, as "one of the first of the domestic dramas of the well-to-do in their own surroundings and with their own problems, presented without moralizing and from their point of view." *The Cheat* was put into production and directed by Cecil B. De Mille, beginning October 20, 1915. With me in the cast were Fannie Ward, Jack Dean and James Neill, who was an actor as well as a director for the Lasky company.

The Cheat was Mr. De Mille's nineteenth picture. In his autobiography, published in 1959, he recalls both it and me, writing: "It was a rather daring theme for its time, the story of a society woman who gambled away Red Cross funds entrusted to her, borrowed $10,000 from a wealthy Japanese in consideration of a promise which was plainly if delicately hinted, then tried to repay her debt in cash instead of keeping her promise. At this point the Japanese branded her on the shoulder with the mark he used to identify all his possessions. The woman shot the Japanese and was saved from imprisonment only when she bared her branded shoulder in open court.

"Told that baldly, the story sounds melodramatic if not lurid. That is why I resolved to direct its acting with great restraint; and I had two highly accomplished artists in the leading roles, Fannie Ward as the woman and Sessue Hayakawa as the Japanese. . . ."

Cecil B. De Mille was thirty-four years old when he directed me in *The Cheat*. The first time I saw him, he had called me to his office for a conference about the picture. I found myself facing a fairly short, balding man with an athletic figure. He was wearing well-tailored light tan riding breeches and a spotlessly clean, white dress shirt. The collar was open, but the cuffs were firmly closed around his wrists by links. Mr. De Mille had a fondness for cufflinks and rings set with stones that matched. He wore leather puttees and high-topped, tightly laced shoes with extra thick heels. His hair was dark and curly and thickly bunched on the back of his head in a strip running from ear to ear. His nose was prominent—not large, however, and straight. He presented a very impressive profile. He had keen eyes and a firm mouth, which with his nose made his face a study in alert determination. All in all, he was a commanding person, even when he was in repose and thinking.

My memory of Mr. De Mille as a person and as a director is by far the strongest I have of making *The Cheat*. Forbidding as he appeared to be at times—and to some people all the time—Mr. De Mille was a patient and understanding man whose job fascinated him, and whose grasp of its essentials and imaginative use of them was phenomenal. It had to be. Six days after he began shooting *The Cheat*, another picture in production in the Selma Avenue studio —*The Golden Chance*, starring Edna Goodrich and Wallace Reid—bogged in trouble and lost its director. Mr. De Mille stepped in to guide it as well as *The Cheat*. He

worked in double harness with the aplomb of a true master
craftsman. He directed Fannie Ward, Jack Dean, James
Neill and me from nine o'clock in the morning straight
through until five in the afternoon. Then, after a short
nap in his office, and dinner on his desk, he directed the
cast of *The Golden Chance* from eight in the evening till
two the following morning. The strain was terrific. I
didn't envy him one bit, particularly when the leading
ladies of both pictures became difficult to work with.

He had trouble first with Fannie Ward. Samuel Goldfish, who represented the Lasky company in New York, had
engaged and sent her to Hollywood. Fannie Ward was a
beautiful and talented woman with a seductive voice and
manner. But she was highly temperamental. Her personality and Mr. De Mille's clashed immediately, and she
walked out and went back to New York to complain about
him to Mr. Goldfish. But just as abruptly as she left she was
back and cast as Mrs. Hardy opposite me in *The Cheat*.

This was her first motion picture, and one would have
thought she would be co-operative. But she wasn't. "The
air on the set was extravagantly cool," a De Mille assistant,
Phil Koury, writes in his book about him; "nor was it
improved much by an accident in the course of filming.
Miss Ward, outfitted in costly ermine and a Parisian gown
and hat, was padding lightly over a footbridge when it
collapsed, chucking the graceful star into three feet of
water."

Fannie Ward also brought her marital problems on the
set. She was married to a very wealthy man who often
visited her at the studio. His appearance seemed a cue of
some sort. Practically every time he dropped by, a fight
would ensue and Fannie would throw things. Their marriage did not last. They parted, and she later married
Jack Dean.

I think Mr. De Mille was very charitable in recalling Fannie Ward. She was a good actress. She had been on the legitimate stage in New York and had excellent technique. But she sorely tried Mr. De Mille's patience. Her performance in *The Cheat* was all he desired. It satisfied him. However, that film was the only De Mille production she was assigned to do.

I don't believe in making excuses for others, especially when it is evident they are wrong and are perfectly capable of doing right. But I do think one of the things that must have brought out Fannie Ward's bad temper was the bright lights we worked under on the closed sets. They were hard on the eyes and, as a result, hard on the nerves. They were carbon lights, and the glare from them was hot and penetrating. Sometimes, after a long stint, our eyes would ache for two or three days and it would be impossible to work. Even today studio lights are rough on the eyes. That they are is one reason motion picture people habitually wear dark glasses.

Mr. De Mille's trouble with the leading lady of *The Golden Chance* was of another kind. Edna Goodrich, a brilliant actress with a record of stage hits both in the United States and Europe, drank; or, as Mr. De Mille reports, could not drink. One night she appeared on the set in a very sorry condition, and he was obliged to choose between her and the picture. Of course, he chose *The Golden Chance*, and replaced her with another actress.

But, for all this burden, Mr. De Mille's ability was not fazed. He completed both pictures on schedule and, without taking a vacation, plunged right on into other projects.

As a director, Mr. De Mille was strong on having an actor understand the motive—on knowing why he must shout or laugh or cry. He liked his action to arise out of genuine emotion. He picked his people very carefully, and, once he selected them, expressed great confidence in them. He allowed his actors to give their own best interpretations of their parts, and only stepped in to advise when it became evident what was being done was out of tune with or opposed to the sweep of the emotional and physical action as he saw it.

He paid me a very kind compliment by mentioning his decision to direct *The Cheat* with restraint and calling me a highly accomplished artist all in the same sentence. Actually, he did not direct me. Now and again he made suggestions, but for the most part he left me alone to go my way according to my own understanding of the role. He only suggested; he did not tell me what to do or tell me how to do it. "All right, Sessue, you do it the way you feel," he would say. And when the cameraman began to shoot the scene Mr. De Mille would lapse into silence. We got along very well. I enjoyed making the picture, and I treasure my memory of having worked for Mr. De Mille.

Mr. De Mille's method of directing, when I worked for him, allowed for my way of acting—the only way I know. I perform a role out of myself as myself, as I feel it, by letting the demands of the character flow from me.

Acting in Hollywood has for years been subject to continual refinement. There was nothing subtle about it in the early days. In their efforts to convey emotions without the assistance of sound, actors' eyes bulged in surprise, in horror and in anger; their mouths gaped and their faces worked grotesquely. "Suppose it were grief," writer Harry Easterfield explained in an interview he had with me in 1918. "The hero must register his heart-stricken woe. So he turns full on the audience, walks toward the camera and allows his facial muscles a bit of exercise. His eyebrows go up, his forehead is wrinkled, his brow is furrowed, the mouth corners turn down, his nose is drawn, and even his ears seem to wiggle in sympathy. . . ."

Harry overdid it somewhat. Such an involved mime reaction provokes laughter, as its use is intended to do when used today to satirize the past. But he is not too far off center.

I found it impossible to act in such a manner. I had to act as I myself would act in real life.

"If I want to show on the screen that I hate a man," I told Harry Easterfield, "I do not shake my fists at him. I think down in my heart how I hate him and try not to move a muscle of my face, just as I would in life."

"Then you get your subtle effects by repression," he theorized.

I smiled. "If you have the teeling, it will come out and the audience will understand, no matter how subtle or delicate the indication."

"But how?"

"I wish I could tell you. But unless you have studied Eastern philosophy, it is hard to make it clear. There are many life forces that the East knows that are not to be put into words."

That is what makes Zen so difficult to explain accurately. Zen has aided me immeasurably in my acting, but since it is something "round and rolling, slippery and slick," as the Chinese say, it is hard to interpret the impact of Zen upon one's actions. I can say, however, that through Zen I have been able to subordinate exterior influences which detract from the sincerity and naturalness of performance.

I believe that in acting the mental attitude must be what is termed as the state of *muga*—an absence of the sense of "I am doing it." Speech and action come from the heart without pausing on the middle ground of intellect. I can best illustrate what I mean with the words of another— one of modern Japan's **greatest** *kendo* swordsmen, Takano

Shigeyoshi, for I often think of my acting roles as swords. Certainly an actor wields a part as a sword, with all the nuance, grace and force of a fencer. Thus Mr. Shigeyoshi explains what I drive at when he writes:

"When I have a bamboo sword most suited to my personal taste . . . I can enter more readily into a state of identity where my body and the sword I hold become one.' . . .

"I sometimes think that when the marionette master puts his mind wholly into the play, his state of mind attains something of the swordsman's. He is then not conscious of the distinction between himself and the doll he manipulates."

So it is with the parts I play. Zen gives me a oneness with them. Through Zen I am able to empty my mind of all thoughts that may hinder my performance. What comes out of me comes intuitively, unconsciously, and everything seems natural.

This manner of acting elicited considerable comment. It was different; and the difference of it was the touchstone of my success. Mr. De Mille did not comprehend the cause, perhaps—I did not discuss the means by which I achieved the ends desired. But he certainly appreciated the effect, and was kind enough to speak later about my "authority and dignity and polished artistry" when writing about my performance in *The Cheat*.

Recalling my experiences in making this picture brings to mind the opposition my playing the role of the villainous Japanese stirred among those of my nationality in Los Angeles and throughout the country after the film was released.

For portraying the heavy, as screen villains are called, as a Japanese, I was indignantly accused of casting a slur on my nationality. "He might have been a Russian, a French-

man, a Spaniard—the nationality didn't count," I explained
to Pearl Gaddis, a writer from *Motion Picture Classic*
magazine, when she asked me about this early in 1916, a
few months after *The Cheat* had made its debut and was
playing throughout the country. "The man was merely a
villain, and a new twist was given the scenario by making
him a Japanese."

The Cheat was an original film scenario written by a
Lasky staff writer, Hector Turnbull, who formerly had
been the dramatic critic of the New York *Tribune*. He
was paid $250 for it. The picture cost $17,000 to make and
netted the Lasky company the largest single picture profit
it had made up to that time, $120,000.

A curious bit of history concerning the scenario is that it
was converted into a play and produced on the stage after
it was produced as a motion picture; and, still later, was
turned into an opera that was performed at the Metro-
politan in New York. This uniqueness has confused film
and theatrical historians. Only recently one, while discussing the picture, referred to the source as a "hackneyed
but powerful old barnstormer," as if the play had come
first. As a matter of further fact, the play did and did not
come first, for after *The Cheat* was turned into a play and
an opera, it was made twice more as a film. I played my
same role in one of the two remakes—a sound version
produced in France more than twenty years after the
original. Mr. Lasky was certainly right when he described
the scenario in his memoirs as a $250 phenomenon. I don't
think any other film script has yielded so much production
mileage.

Mr. De Mille also remarks about the screen-to-stage
journey of *The Cheat* in his autobiography. He points out
that it "was the first motion picture to be later made into
a stage play." And he also writes: "It was also Sessue

Hayakawa's first giant stride on the road that made him within two years the peer of such contemporary bright stars as Douglas Fairbanks, William S. Hart, and Mary Pickford."

On the other hand, Jesse Lasky, in his memoirs, says the picture made me a star. Mr. De Mille's observation, however, is the truer.

In any event *The Cheat* gave a terrific boost to the progress of the career in motion pictures that I began with *Typhoon* and *The Wrath of the Gods.*

Throughout 1916, when *The Cheat* was released, 1917, and 1918, the public saw quite a bit of me on the screen. I made *Alien Souls, The Victorian Cross,* and *The Clue,* in 1916; *The Bottle Imp, The Jaguar's Claws, Each to His Kind; Forbidden Paths, Hashimura Togo, His Honorable Friend, The City of Dim Faces,* and *The Soul of Kura san,* in 1917; *The Secret Game, Hidden Pearls, The Call of the East, The Honor of His House,* and *The Bravest Way,* in 1918.

In these pictures and others I was able to dispel the deep-stained conception of the Oriental as a man of mystery and a traditionally sinister figure. The outbreak of World War I led to a new policy regarding all minorities, according to Lewis Jacobs. "Likewise," he writes, "the 'yellow peril' agitation against the Japanese and Chinese disappeared from the screen, since these groups were now with the Allies. The Japanese were represented not only humanly and sympathetically but romantically. Especially significant was the rise of the Japanese actor Sessue Hayakawa. He became one of the leading stars of the day, combining culture, sensitivity, exotic handsomeness, and refinement."

Along these same lines, Deems Taylor points out: "Sessue Hayakawa became the only Oriental actor ever to play romantic leads in American pictures. Because of racial prejudices, however, he always had to relinquish the girl in the final reel."

Mr. Jacobs and Mr. Taylor honor me. All I can say here is, I did my best. Public acceptance of me in romantic roles was a blow of sorts against racial intolerance, even though I lost the girl in the last reel. By and large, I have never been bothered by racial prejudice; and I have never paid much attention to it. I'm sure if I did, I would find it. One can always find hatred, distrust and trouble if one expressly looks for them.

After *The Cheat* I made *Alien Souls*, the film which brought my wife to the screen. Thereafter, working for the Lasky company, she played in quite a number of my pictures and developed into a film favorite herself. Incidentally, it was in *Alien Souls* that I was seen in one of my sympathetic roles, and one which helped redeem me with those who damned me for my portrayal in *The Cheat*.

In my pictures I often played a Japanese or a Chinese; but, thankfully for artistic reasons, not all of the time. In *The Jaguar's Claws,* for instance, I performed the role of a Mexican—a man with a character like Juarez, subtle in his general conduct, rational, but stern, and when pressed, vicious. I liked the part very much.

The motion picture business, by the time I made *The Jaguar's Claws* in mid-1917, had become big business—as big as the dreams had been of the men who had recognized the potential of films and established the industry not much more than a decade before. I allude to men such as Adolph Zukor, Jesse L. Lasky, Samuel Goldwyn, Cecile B. De Mille, Carl Laemmle, D. W. Griffith, William Fox and William Selig. These names stand out, as do those of Mack Sennett and Thomas H. Ince. These were some of the leading figures behind the cameras and the scenes. Pictures were making them very rich in 1917. Studios were bigger, production schedules were longer and salaries were steadily climbing. My studio had been merged with Mr. Zukor's company and was now known as Famous Players-Lasky. Carl Laemmle had opened Universal in Culver City. Inceville was a busy place. First National had been organized and was making films with two of the biggest stars of all time, Mary Pickford and Charlie Chaplin. The landscape around Los Angeles was dotted with studios, and picture people had become a substantial part of the population, physically and economically.

The winter of 1917 a man appeared out of my past to change the course of my life again. My old college friend William Connery arrived in Los Angeles with his parents and sisters and, learning that Kintaro Hayakawa and Sessue Hayakawa were one and the same person, he telephoned me at home and invited me to meet him at his hotel for a drink or two and some talk about old times in Chicago. He afterward took me to meet his family and some other people who expressed considerable interest in the motion picture business.

One of the men I met through Bill Connery was named Dohrman. He was a millionaire, a man who had made his fortune in a chain of china and glassware stores. Bill Connery sketched him as a keen judge of character and a man to impress. We had dinner together—Bill and his family, Mr. Dohrman, Tsuru and I—and the following day Bill paid me a visit and abruptly asked me, "Why don't you start your own motion picture company, instead of working for Paramount?" By this time everybody called the studios in the distributing group Paramount.

"My own company!"

"Sure, why not?" Bill said. "How long have you got to go with your contract with Paramount?"

The idea of having my own film company flabbergasted

me. I had secretly nurtured thoughts of writing and directing in addition to acting, but had never taken any definite steps to do so. "I have another six months to go," I told him. "Why?"

"Don't renew your contract, Sessue. Don't sign. Start your own company instead."

The idea was appealing, but I thought he was joking and said so. He frowned. "No, I'm not joking," Bill assured me. "I mean what I say. We'll give you the money to start."

"We?"

"My parents and I," he said. "Look, I told you Mr. Dohrman was a good judge of character. He made quite a study of you at dinner last night. He has faith in you. My parents and I do, too. You certainly realize your value to Paramount. You've been kept pretty busy there. Tsuru, too. Think what you can do on your own."

I did think about it. I thought about the idea considerably after asking Bill to give me four or five days' time. He chuckled. "You wouldn't be you if you moved any sooner, Sessue. Take your time. If you say yes, it will take some months to organize anyway, so don't worry about not completing your contract with Paramount."

"When you say you'll give me the money to start, Bill . . ."

"My parents are willing to advance one million dollars," he interrupted. "You've only to say yes."

"One million dollars," I exclaimed. "Now I know I'm going to think about this!"

Bill Connery left then, and I explained the proposition he had laid before me and the possibilities of it to Tsuru. The idea of being given one million dollars with which to produce our own pictures was an overwhelming one.

During the next week I consulted close friends in the business and asked their views on the idea of going into producing my own films. The majority thought it a sound one and considered me quite fortunate to have it thrust on me. At length, I agreed and told Bill Connery and his parents that, "Yes, I would like to have my own company."

"We're off then," Bill said. He proceeded to organize on paper against the day when my contract with Paramount would expire.

My entry into the business was significant of a trend which developed as the film industry expanded in general. "Stars began forming their own production companies," Lewis Jacobs has written. "If an actor or actress incorporated, it was a sign of success. William S. Hart, Anita Stewart, Norma Talmadge, Charles Chaplin, Douglas Fairbanks, Charles Ray, Clara Kimball Young, Sessue Hayakawa, Roscoe Arbuckle, Frank Keenan, and Agnes Ayres were a few of the many notables who flung themselves into production."

Backed by $1,000,000, banked in my name as promised by the Connerys, my independent motion picture production company was organized and announced in March, 1918. I named it the Haworth Pictures Corporation. I was still engaged in making pictures for Famous Players-Lasky, and about to go on location in Hawaii to film *Hidden Pearls*; so the first few months of my incorporation were given over to paper work, the acquisition of a studio, employment of a staff and the hiring of a company of players. I purchased D. W. Griffith's old studio on Sunset Boulevard, close to where Paramount Studios are located today. I paid $300,000 for it, and invested another large amount in equipping its four stages with lights, cameras and the thousand and one other necessities of film making.

Then I engaged William Worthington and James Young to direct. With them, I laid out an immediate production schedule of two pictures, *His Birthright* and *The Temple of Dusk,* both of which we selected, according to a trade-paper report, "as being the most effective vehicle for [my] talents and containing dramatic elements that will appeal most strongly to the public taste at the present time."

Unlike comedian Charles Ray who went into independent production bent upon creating a new image of himself—and lost a fortune trying—I was not about to change away from the type of picture which had earned me my fame and following. We announced these pictures for September, 1918, release, and contracted to have them and the rest of our output distributed through the exchanges of the Mutual Film Corporation. "In these first productions and others which are to follow," I said in a press release, "I am happy to say I will have splendid opportunity for the kind of acting which most appeals to me and, I am sure, makes the most profound impression upon the audience—the repressive, natural kind, devoid of gesticulation and heroics."

His Birthright, an original story by Dennison Clift, was the first film produced under the Haworth banner. I cast myself and Tsuru in it, and from the crowd of actors and actresses which answered our first casting call selected Marian Sais and Howard Davis to join us. Marian, I recall, gave up a serial contract which might well have put her in the same league with Pearl White. Howard Davis was a stock actor who entered films from vaudeville.

Although we planned to make eight pictures a year after our initial two, we ended by producing eleven features in 1919, the first full year of operations. These included *Heart in Pawn, Gray Horizon, Courageous Coward, Bonds of Honor, The Dragon Painter,* and *House of Intrigue,* for which I engaged a third director, Lloyd Ingraham. Lloyd, Bill Worthington and Jim Young directed all scenes except the ones in which I appeared. I preferred to direct those myself.

My Haworth corporation operated for about four years. We made twenty-three pictures in all, and employed, among others, Dagmar Godowsky, Jane Novak, Helen Eddy, Bessie Love, and Colleen Moore; and a number of Japanese actors and actresses, including Togo Yamamoto, Michi Konishi, Misao Seki, and my old friend Toyo Fujita. Jean Acker, when she worked for me, was married to a handsome, soulful young man named Rodolpho Alfonzo Rafaelo Pierre Filibert Guglielmi di Valentina d'Antonguolla, whose first picture was shortly to catapult him to stardom. His professional name was Rudolph Valentino. The film was *The Four Horsemen of the Apocalypse.*

Valentino was among those who had applied for work when Haworth began production. I met him then, and liked him; but I did not hire him. The atmosphere of his personality was too similar to mine. And although his acting ability was less than skin deep, I sensed something of a rival in him. He once paid me the compliment of saying, "I've always wanted to have something of the art you achieve in your performances in mine, so I could reproduce the sort of action and behavior the public associates with you."

When I agreed to form my own company, I really didn't comprehend what I was letting myself in for. Tsuru and I were living comfortably in a bungalow in Hollywood, and were devoting our off hours to simple pleasures—reading and the like—which allowed us to retreat from the demanding rush of our work. But for me, all that disappeared as Haworth got rolling. Almost overnight, I was constantly at the studio concocting scenarios, drafting production plans, directing, checking the rushes, editing and supervising everything. I found myself working as much as twenty hours a day. I quickly realized why I hadn't envied

Mr. De Mille when he had been forced to direct two
pictures at once.

Finally, by 1920, the pace had become too much. I cut
our production in half and attempted to live a little.

Also, we ran afoul of Los Angeles fire law in 1920. It
became necessary to get a new studio. The old Griffith
plant, made mostly of wood, was condemned as a fire
hazard.

About this time a new production and distribution company, Robertson-Cole, was organized by a group of British
and American film investors. The president, Rufus Cole,
invited me to consolidate my company, Haworth Pictures
Corporation, with it. Robertson-Cole built a completely
new and generally fireproof studio, so I accepted Mr. Cole's
offer and moved my base of operations.

My association with Robertson-Cole continued my success
as an independent producer. After four years of movie-
making Haworth showed a net profit of more than two
million dollars over and above the one million dollar
investment in me made by the Connerys, whom I was able to
repay, with interest, after three years.

My reduced production schedule and the consolidation
with Robertson-Cole gave Tsuru and me a chance to slack
off and relax a bit. We moved out of our bungalow and
into a three-story mansion surrounded by a broad expanse
of lawn. The mansion was on the corner of Franklin Street
and Argyle Avenue. It became a regular stop on the sight-
seeing bus route around Hollywood.

I purchased the house when it was still being built. When
completed, it looked like a castle complete with a tower
and battlements. It was quite a showplace, right in step
with the times. Prohibition had come, and like everyone
else in Hollywood in the financial position to do so, I
hedged against the drought by buying a railroad carload

of liquor. I had it brought west from Chicago. The era of the "wild party" was under way in the film colony. Tsuru and I were obliged to entertain on a large and lavish scale. My success and our position demanded that we do so. It was part of belonging, one of those things you are expected to do when your lives become enmeshed in so vast an enterprise, social as well as professional, as motion pictures.

The parties we gave were generally successful, happy gatherings. We were popular, and people enjoyed visiting us. However, I don't think we were *that* popular. I think the wine cellar was. Along with Roscoe Arbuckle and a dress manufacturer named Vic Levy, our stock was one of the best in Hollywood.

I went "Hollywood" as the term is for another reason, too. An anti-Japanese feeling had begun to take hold in California. There was talk of legislation to prohibit Orientals from owning property, and eventually such a law was passed. It was not repealed until after World War II. Such agitation angered me. So it was not just out of vanity and the demand of social obligation that I acquire "Argyle Castle" as our mansion was promptly nicknamed. Defiantly, I was determined to show the Americans who surrounded me that I, a Japanese, could live up to their lavish standards. Along with the mansion, I took up golf and became an avid player, frequently held poker parties— and frequently lost—and I purchased a number of automobiles. At one time I had four: two Cadillacs, a Ford and a Pierce Arrow town sedan for all of which I paid something like $12,000.

Hollywood at this time, as the postwar excitement heightened and the boom of the 1920's began, entertained itself at gigantic parties given in rotation by the top stars, producers and directors. Until Prohibition flushed speakeasies and drinking clubs into existence there were few such places in Hollywood. A lot of the picture people made it a habit to gather at the old Alexandria Hotel, the Ambassador, and restaurants such as Al Levy's.

But the real social gatherings took place in the big homes and rambling gardens that sprang up throughout the Hollywood area, dotting the hills and canyons and the not too distant seashore, before Beverly Hills became the focal point of stars' residences. William S. Hart, Tom Mix, Mary Pickford, Douglas Fairbanks, Roscoe "Fatty" Arbuckle, Buster Keaton, Frances X. Bushman, Gloria Swanson, Charlie Chaplin, and Marion Davies were only a few of the stars earning weekly salaries in four and five figures who built manor houses with grounds rivaling the ducal establishments of feudal France and England.

Argyle Castle, large as it was, was a tract home compared to the estate Marion Davies built, and at which she entertained what seemed like half of the film colony at one party. Ocean House, she called it, and she spent seven million dollars building it. Pickfair, built after Mary Pickford and Douglas Fairbanks were married in March, 1920, was another dazzling home. So was the place Charlie Chaplin built on a hilltop after having the top planed flat. The newspapers reported he spent three million on it.

Stars' and directors' parties were the main source of after work relaxation and having fun at this time. They were not all wild, uninhibited affairs at which we stripped off our clothing and swam naked in the swimming pool or disappeared into the nearest bedroom to take narcotics and someone else's wife. This is what the same public which made us rich and famous wanted to believe, however, and every now and then at some party we would catch a photographer hiding in the shrubbery hoping to take the sort of pictures which would prove the public was right.

Regardless of the reports, there were more wild parties seen in Cecil B. De Mille's pictures, the ones he made during the first half of the Roaring Twenties, and in those of Erich Von Stroheim, than were held in real life. However, I cannot deny that nothing happened. Things did. Roscoe Arbuckle held a party in his hotel suite in San Francisco in the fall of 1921 and his career came to an end when a guest at the party died a few days after he supposedly raped her. Less than six months after this scandal smote the film colony, William Desmond Taylor, chief director for Famous Players-Lasky, was mysteriously murdered in the study of his Hollywood home. The killer has never been found. The murder opened a flood of hearsay and gossip that ruined two more film careers, those of Mabel Normand and beautiful Mary Miles Minter. Then, in 1923, handsome Wallace Reid who had risen to fabulous stardom since making *The Golden Chance*, succumbed to dope addiction and died, a pitifully wasted shell of a man.

These were isolated instances, terrible ones, but not typical. Nevertheless, they gave Hollywood the greatest black eye it has ever received, and brought down the public wrath which ended in the organization of the Hays Office.

Lots of money—having it and spending it—seems eventually to foster such evil. What certain people do with their money, especially if they have great wealth, is always of consuming interest to others. What was done with the millions of dollars made in motion pictures during my Hollywood career was the subject of thousands of words in print and speech. Many of the great stars of the silent era put their money to work for good causes and spent wisely. But such pursuits are never as interesting to readers and listeners as tales of mass drunkenness, sex orgies, dope addiction, and all the other accounts of debauchery circulated about motion picture people during the years I was extensively active in Hollywood.

But far from being the sort of wild gathering a few well-publicized affairs made typical in the public mind was the sort of party Tsuru and I gave at Argyle Castle. We sometimes invited two hundred and fifty to dinner and had six hundred to tea, as we called our cocktail gatherings after Prohibition took over. Such affairs cost me four or five thousand dollars—less than a week's income.

The money came and went. I earned a large income and lived in a manner befitting my earnings. I did not effect a habit of spending on a large scale—like Mae Marsh, for instance; but my tastes did not allow me to be miserly. I did not covet the grandeur we lived in, but enjoyed it and did not attach too much importance to whether it would last or end. I tried to follow the middle road. The middle road is best. And it is the way of the Buddha, who did not either stress austerity or condone immersion in worldly pleasures.

My life in Hollywood was not gaudy, it was happy. Hollywood was a happy place then. People were more friendly, open in their dealings and in their display of affection. The atmosphere was more like that surrounding a happy hard-working family. But as the picture industry grew and grew more, when sound came to transform it into even bigger business, and to shatter the careers of those whose voices could never be their fortunes, the personalness slowly faded and died. The gaiety and the excitement disappeared. Today I envy those times. I miss them.

"Many are the screen idols who have served their time in the hospitals this summer." This observation appeared in an article which appeared in the September, 1921, issue of *Motion Picture Classic*. "The most unusual case of all is Sessue Hayakawa, the celebrated Japanese actor," the author, Kenneth McGaffey, remarked.

In the spring of 1921, I was working on a picture entitled *The Swamp* with Bessie Love, Frankie Lee and Harland Tucker. J. G. Alexander had written the scenario from a story I wrote. Colin Campbell was directing.

This picture was being made by the Robertson-Cole company. The integration of the Haworth Pictures Corporation into Robertson-Cole, begun in 1920 when we changed studios, was almost complete. The only problem left to solve concerned the transfer of my million dollars of life insurance from my company, the original beneficiary, to Robertson-Cole.

In a way, the plot of *The Swamp* foreshadowed what was to happen to me in real life.

My role in this picture was that of a Chinese vegetable peddler. The setting was lower east side New York. Bessie Love played a slum girl, secretly the object of my affections. She is taken severely ill, and the peddler undertakes to provide for her care. She does not respond to treatment, however; and as she sinks lower and lower toward death, she agrees to a marriage with the peddler so he can watch over her in the after-life. Following a bedside ceremony, the peddler conveys to the dying girl's almost unconscious mind the joy of his possession of her in marriage. His happiness sparks her will to live, and she recovers, brought back to life and health by the constant vigil and faith of the peddler. I acted to express the peddler's strength of mind and power of will, not knowing that I would have to employ both in sustaining my own life.

For while the picture was being made I was struck down by severe pains in my abdomen. At first I thought my old wounds were to blame. But a medical examination revealed I was suffering from an appendicitis attack.

Against my doctor's advice I continued to work on the picture. I got sicker by the day, and finally reached a point where I was applying ice-packs to my side between scenes in an effort to hold up until the film was finished. More interested in protecting their investment than they were in my health, the management of Robertson-Cole made a strong case out of what my withdrawal from the picture would mean in financial terms of production delay. At the same time, Robertson-Cole pressed its demand for my life insurance. I later learned they had entertained the idea of cashing in if they got it and I died.

The same stubbornness that ultimately cost me my naval career characterized my attitude about my appendix. I kept working until it ruptured, and I finished the picture. Then I was rushed from the studio to the hospital and into the operating room. The doctors did their job, but didn't offer too much encouragement. The burst appendix had pretty well poisoned my system. My recovery was left to me. The battle for life was purely mental. I concentrated on living, bending my will through Zen, refusing to let go. I thought of Eichi and my lonely months on the mountain, and added my will to the efforts of my doctors, and won. I recovered.

I was released from the hospital the middle of June. After a few days at home I went to Washington, D. C., where I was received at the White House by President Harding.

From Washington I went to Boyle's Thirty Acres in Jersey City, New Jersey, where I watched Jack Dempsey defend and retain his heavyweight boxing championship by knocking out Georges Carpentier of France, in the fourth round of their fight on July 2, 1921. I had expressed a wish to see the fight prior to being taken ill while filming *The Swamp*. After I pulled through, the talk around Hollywood was that I had refused to die without seeing it. This, of course, made good newspaper copy.

It was on the way to New York from Washington that I met a comedian named Sam S———. He did not have a hat, so in a sudden burst of generosity I bought him one. It was a hot day, and I felt sorry for him. No sooner had he put the hat on, however, than it blew off and into a muddy ditch. I told him to leave it, but Sam insisted on wearing it dirt and all. He and I went to the fight together, and once, when he left his seat—and the hat, I amused myself by signing my name on it. Someone saw me do this, and four or five other famous people signed the hat. In a twinkling, Sam's hat became a collector's item. After the fight, he was asked to sell it, but refused. "Sessue bought this hat for me," he said. "I could use the money, but I can't sell it."

The idea that the hat was worth money because of the signatures on it impressed Sam no end. He decided to increase its value to getting more autographs on it. The signatures of Will Rogers, Valentino, and Henry Ford were some he was able to collect. It took him eight years to get Henry Ford's name on the hat.

Sam's dirty hat has become quite famous. Today it is insured for thousands of dollars, and I understand Sam has been making money by displaying the hat.

Such a result was the last thing I could have had in mind when I wrote my name on the hat, but time has proved that my impulsive action, taken because it amused me, was a seed of kindness. Some are bad, some are good, and the planter stands or falls by their harvest. The history of the hat is a good example.

The idea that I recovered from my illness because I was determined to be on hand for the Dempsey-Carpentier championship fight made a good story. The newspapers and motion picture magazines made much of it. But the story was nothing in comparison to what could have been written about what took place after I saw the fight and returned to Hollywood to begin work on another Robertson-Cole film, *The Vermilion Pencil*, which proved to be my last picture in Hollywood until I made my first "talkie" in 1933.

Written by Homer Lee and directed by Norman Dawn, *The Vermilion Pencil* was a romantic thriller laid in China. My co-star in it was Bessie Love.

The final scene of the picture was a spectacular one. An earthquake destroyed the Chinese village home of the lovers in the story. It was a breath-taking sequence, dangerous to film. My role called for me to take considerable physical risk. So another million dollars of life insurance was placed on my life. This was done at the suggestion and insistence of the president of Robertson-Cole, not Rufus Cole, but a successor.

Production of *The Vermilion Pencil* moved swiftly and smoothly after it began early in 1922. The film colony was still in the throes of recovering from the blow it received when Roscoe Arbuckle was arrested and charged with the rape manslaughter of Virginia Rappe, a young bit player and hanger-on who was a guest at his party in San Francisco. Hard work and no play seemed to be everyone's attitude.

Work on *The Vermilion Pencil* reached the wrap-up stage. We began to shoot the final scene—that of a gun and fist fight between me and three other actors, ending when the earthquake hit.

We had filmed the gun fight sequence earlier. I had been chased to a wall and while I pressed my back against it and waited for the worst, five shots had been lined in about my head from off camera by an expert hired for the job. I cannot explain why, but this scene had worried me. I had been compelled to draw the expert to one side before shooting the scene. I wanted to learn his feelings about me. Not me, actually, but about Japanese. The agitation against us was still prevalent, and those of small income, engaged in farming and small business in California, were having a hard time of it. This man smiled when I expressed my concern. "Don't give it another thought," he assured me. "If you remain where you're blocked to stand, Mr. Hayakawa, all you'll feel is a little wind."

I had to test him. Daring myself, I put a cigarette in my mouth and stood against one of the concrete walls erected for the village set. He took aim, fired and clipped the cigarette neatly out of my lips. I had him do this four more times before returning to the set and going on with the scene.

This time, however, as the earthquake scene got under way, my worry was more fear. Something was definitely wrong. There were more visitors on the set than usual.

"It is quite a gallery, isn't it?" Norman Dawn said when I pointed the extra people out to him. "Scenes like this one always gather a crowd. Human nature. People like to see stuff like fires and earthquakes. All set?" he called, and walked away.

In this scene I was called upon to fight beneath the overhang of a large building topped with a pagoda. Both the building and the pagoda were real—constructed of concrete and stone. They had been mined with dynamite, and when the earthquake was signaled by the director they would be sent crashing—away from us, I was told. But when the other three actors and I took our positions for the fight, the set director called me aside.

He cupped his hand to his mouth near my ear. "Whatever you do, Sessue, don't fight near the pagoda."

"Why not?" I stared at him.

"Because it's rigged to fall on you, not away. I made it,

and I know it won't fall away. When that thing starts to come down, run. Otherwise, you'll—well . . ."

"I understand." I turned to look at the president of the company. He had joined observers from the insurance company to watch this scene. He stood to gain the most if the pagoda fell on me.

The idea that my death would be plotted under circumstances like these seemed absurd. Norman Dawn had assured me the pagoda would collapse in the earthquake without endangering me or the others. But the set director's warning confirmed the sense of uneasiness I felt when I arrived to play.

As we took our positions for the fight scene I warned my companions, "The pagoda is supposed to fall down on the far side, but you can never tell. If I suddenly yell, 'Run!' while we're fighting, break off and run. I don't want to take chances any more than you do."

We began to fight. After a few minutes I heard the pistol shot signaling the earthquake. It was followed by a thunderous roar. The wall next to us began to buckle. I looked up at the pagoda. It was coming down on us.

"Run!" I yelled and plunged toward the camera. The other actors scattered, dodging the falling wood and brick. Luckily, none of us was hurt.

When the last of the buildings had finished toppling and the dust cleared, I walked over to the president of the company and stared at him. "You nearly got your wish," I told him. "Too bad I didn't die!" He paled and turned away.

This attempt on my life took place in early March, 1922. On the seventeenth of the month the executives of Robertson-Cole held a dinner to celebrate the completion of *The Vermilion Pencil* and the progress of the company.

I was present, and when I was invited to speak, said:

"Thanks to your support I have become a successful star in motion pictures. The other day, a public poll was taken concerning the current discrimination against Japanese in this country and the passage of legislation that will do them considerable harm. I have learned that this company has taken a position in favor of discrimination against the Japanese. Moreover, an attempt on my life was made during the filming of *The Vermilion Pencil*. Fortunately for me it was unsuccessful. I was warned.

"If things have reached such a state, there is no longer any cause for me to remain in Hollywood. I am going to leave. This is my last day."

There was not a single word uttered by those present when I finished and sat down. The president of Robertson-Cole stared vacantly at his fingernails. His face was ashen.

The attempt to murder me for my insurance ended my activities as an independent film producer, and suspended my participation in American motion pictures for a period of ten years. I disposed of my business interests, sold all my automobiles except the Pierce Arrow and closed up Argyle Castle. Later, in 1925, I presented the house to a group of Jewish friends and acquaintances. They converted its spacious twenty-six rooms into a synagogue. Argyle Castle was still standing and in use when I returned to Hollywood in 1949 to make *Tokyo Joe*, my first post-World War II film. It has since been razed to make way for one of Hollywood's numerous freeways.

Now a completely free agent, I concentrated on two things: a visit to Japan and to New York, where I hoped to return to stage acting and appear on Broadway. Toward accomplishing the first, Tsuru and I sailed for Yokohama from San Francisco shortly after our eighth wedding anniversary, May 1, 1922. I went happily, having cleansed my mind of the evil thoughts which gripped it following the murder attempt. It was not for me to indulge in retribution. Evil only begets evil. In time, the man who plotted to kill me reaped in ratio to what he had sowed. He greedily invested in foreign film stocks and attempted to undersell the American market. But the domestic producers lowered their prices and wiped him out. He died penniless and forgotten.

8   Water in the Hands

Tsuru and I spent a month in Japan. Our journey was a sentimental one, taken to see our families—her aunts and uncles, my brothers and sisters. My elder brother was then governor of Chiba Prefecture, and head of the Hayakawas. My mother had died in 1920.

We landed at Yokohama, and from there went by train to the Boso Peninsula and Nanaura. A large crowd, gathered beneath an arch of welcome, met us at the station; and as I acknowledged the bows and words of welcome, my eyes caught a familiar face peering from behind a grimy station window. It was Tora, my deaf and dumb companion, a boy when I left Japan, now a man grown husky from fishing the waters of the Nanaura coast. His hands snapped words at me, and once again he cried as we renewed our friendship. Then he was gone, swallowed by the crowd which pressed about us as we went to the car my brother had waiting to take us to my father's house.

I never saw Tora again. During the years we had passed together when I was young I had worked with him to kill his shame at being deaf and dumb and develop a compensating pride. "Have courage," I told Tora. "You are more noble than many. Have pride." He believed what I told him, and came to master the frustration of his handicap. As a fisherman he did very well, and in his class became quite wealthy. His pride, though, mounted out of proportion. About two years after I last saw him he was brought down when a slattern in a sake house on one of the small islands off the coast insulted and ridiculed him. She spit in his face and called him a tongueless fool. His humiliation drove his emotions to the wall and he committed hara-kiri with a butcher knife.

The car provided by my brother took us to the gate from which my carriage had taken me away more than a dozen years before.

"I welcome you home, Kintaro," my brother said.

A servant opened the door and we got out and stood for a moment where my parents had stood when I saw them for the last time.

"I have a reception planned, Kintaro," my brother said as we walked from the gate toward the main house. "The newsreels are here and will want pictures first, however."

We crossed the porch and entered the house, going to the living room, after we had removed our shoes and donned slippers. And as I entered the living room the years I had been away were eclipsed by a vision which to this day I do not know if I really saw or just imagined. When, as a boy, I returned from school in Tokyo or a holiday some distance from home, my parents always greeted me formally. They did not come to the front door when I returned, but waited upon me in the living room. I would enter and bow, and I did so now. For I saw them both clearly as I entered the living room. Perhaps it was a hallucination, imagination fulfilling a deep desire. Perhaps . . . I only know that I saw them and that they smiled. The newsreels commented that I greeted my ancestors, the brave Hayakawas who fought beside the Genji; but I greeted my parents when I bowed and knelt. When I looked up they were gone.

True, it seemed impossible. The emotion of returning might well have made my mind play a trick, create the images of my mother and father only in my mind's eye. I told those of my family who gathered to welcome me about what I saw, but they said nothing. But later, when I went to Eichi's temple the priest there nodded in belief and said, "They still love you." Then he told me of Eichi's death and we talked of my life in America and of Zen. And before I left to return to the United States I gave the temple gifts of lanterns to mark the gate.

It is always so when one returns to the scene of childhood. I walked about Nanaura as I had when a boy. In time, I went to visit the temple on the mountain. It had not changed. No one had been there, I thought, since I had been there. The temple looked as it had when I struggled to find myself within the surrounding silence and when I had fled down the mountain after the *Dakota* struck Devil's Rock.

A month passed. Our visit came to an end, and once again I left my father's house. Not once while we were there did I venture near the building where I had attempted to commit suicide. I could not bear to step within its walls nor let my mind too long dwell upon thoughts of what had happened there.

Before we left Japan, Tsuru and I entertained my family at the Imperial Hotel in Tokyo. I remarked to my brother how strong and different from Japanese architecture the

hotel was, and learned from him that Frank Lloyd **Wright**
had designed it. The building, of course, was uniquely to
withstand the great earthquake of 1923.

Following the family reunion celebration we held, Tsuru
and I sailed for San Francisco, and from there went to New
York to carry out the plans I had made previous to putting
Hollywood behind me.

Summer was over when we arrived in New York. The
theatre season was getting under way. And in the fall of
1922 New York theatre was glittering with great names.
Marilyn Miller was starring in *Sally* with Leon Errol and
Walter Catlett, both of whom later became film favorites.
Eugene O'Neill had two plays on Broadway, *The Emperor
Jones* and *The Hairy Ape*. David Belasco was presenting
David Warfield in a revival of *The Merchant of Venice*.
Motion pictures were tremendously popular, but vaude-
ville was still pleasing the thousands who attended The
Palace and The Hippodrome, Loew's State and The Capi-
tol. And, of course, *Abie's Irish Rose* was playing. Despite
the derision of the critics it would play five more years.

I arrived in New York determined to appear in a play.
Lee Shubert put me under contract and brought me together with playwright Fred De Gresac and her romantic
drama, *Tiger Lily*, a mild sort of thriller laid in Chinatown
in San Francisco. (Yes, the playwright was female.)

The lady and I worked on the script together to tailor
it to my needs. To get some peace and quiet we left New
York and went to work in a hotel across the river in New
Jersey. We devoted ourselves exclusively to the play until
one evening the manager of the hotel dropped by my room
to urge me to take a rest and relax by going to dinner at an
Italian restaurant operated by a friend of his. I did so,
and the next thing I knew I was in the middle of a game

of roulette and losing heavily. I drank too much and went to sleep during the game, and when I awoke—still in my chair at the gaming table—I had lost close to $30,000. Since I was in no position to argue, I wrote three checks to cover that amount and returned to New York to see my lawyer and a doctor. I had come to with a terrific headache which the doctor later told me was the result of being drugged. I told my lawyer this and he stopped payment of the checks.

Three days later, three men called on me to ask, "The bank refuses to honor your checks—why?"

I faked surprise. "I don't know anything about that," I said. The visitors then invited me to call the bank, and I did. The manager informed me he didn't know who had stopped the checks. I hung up and explained to my visitors that my lawyer must have done it.

"Then you better phone your lawyer, Hayakawa. One way or another, we want those checks cashed."

I called the lawyer. Fortunately he was not in his office. I told the men to come back later. They did so the following day.

In the meantime, my lawyer advised me to tell them: "When I returned from gambling, I didn't feel too well. So I went to the doctor. He told me I had been drugged and probably was out cold when I lost so much. He has offered to be a witness for me." I smiled. "Now, if you want to call my lawyer . . ." I'm sure consideration was given, for a moment, to the idea of beating the money out of me; but after a short silence the men left. I'm pleased to say they did not return.

However, that experience was not the only one I had with the underworld. Not long after, I went to a speakeasy on New York's lower east side, and over my protests was served champagne and billed $300 for it. I wrote a check, left and felt lucky at getting off so cheap. The next morning my bank called and asked me to approve payment of a check for not three hundred but $2,300. "I remember writing only three hundred," I said. "Have whoever has presented the check wait until I see if I'm mistaken." Of course, my check had been raised; and when there was a delay in payment the person with the check disappeared.

Fred De Gresac and I worked *Tiger Lily* into shape, and it opened outside New York. Supporting me in it were Fay Courteney, Leslie King, Quid Paulson and Mary Carroll. Unfortunately, it was not too good a play. We presented *Tiger Lily* in Philadelphia, Pittsburgh, Atlantic City and Washington, D.C., and though I received good critical reviews of my acting, the play suffered. Lee Shubert decided against bringing it into New York and closed it early in 1923.

I looked for a new play. But before I could find one an offer came from France for me to make a film. Vandal-Delac Studios in Paris had acquired the screen rights of *Croix de Fer,* a novel of the Russo-Japanese War, and its New York representative asked me to play the part of a young lieutenant on Admiral Togo's staff. I accepted, and Tsuru and I sailed for Le Havre on the luxury liner *Ile de France* in January 1923.

Croix de Fer as a film was called *La Bataille* and, when shown in the United States, *The Danger Line*. Both my wife and I had leading roles, along with Cady Winter, F. Ford and Gina Palerme.

But I almost didn't make the picture. It was to be about one of the greatest naval battles of the war, but when I read the script the only mention of a ship was in a scene where I, as Togo's officer, would stand on the bridge of a battleship—a fake, thirty or forty feet long, to be built in the Paris studio—glaring defiantly at the approaching enemy fleet (not one ship of which would be shown, of course) and say, via title, "Japan's future depends upon the winning of this battle."

"Where are the ships?" I asked the producer at our first script conference. "No marine scenes are indicated here." I drew my thumb across the script, riffling the pages.

"They'll be sets in the studio. Mock-ups."

"You mean to tell me I'm going to stand on a fake deck and that will be it?" I looked at him in wonder and thought about the great lengths gone to in Hollywood to achieve atmosphere and impact. The gigantic sets D. W. Griffith had had built and the elaborateness of Von Stroheim's scenery, for examples. Even in my own studio I had not been too economical in getting the effects I desired.

The producer noded and began to look apologetic.

"I read this speech and the guns will fire and everything shakes?" I said, doubt creeping into my voice.

"That's the best we can do, Mr. Hayakawa. The audiences will just have to use their imaginations."

"No fleet," I said, half to myself.

"No," he said, and changed the subject.

I sat through the rest of the conference in silence. And this picture is calculated to be a French masterpiece, I thought. The lack of ships and authentic battle scenes disturbed me greatly. The more I thought about it the more I thought of purchasing passage back to New York.

"I'm sorry," I said just before the conference broke up. "Something will have to be done about the marine scenes. I don't see much sense in making a picture about the Russo-Japanese War, making Togo's fleet a major element and not showing the battles. You're going to have to do better than you have so far or I think I will not do the picture at all."

I left the producer and the director to think over my ultimatum.

Production on *La Bataille* lagged after I said what I felt, so I took to making the rounds of what Paris had to offer.

Paris in 1923 was just getting under way as a mecca for Americans. Tourism from the United States had not yet hit its stride. It would in 1925. Still, the core of the atmosphere of exile still strongly associated with Paris— the American writers, painters and other men and women of the arts—was present when I arrived. I don't recall seeing or meeting any one of the many who later became famous, Ernest Hemingway, F. Scott Fitzgerald, Ezra Pound —they were just names overheard now and then at the parties I attended. We moved in different worlds. The Paris I knew in the 1920's was not the Paris they knew.

One of my diversions while I waited for something to be done about my demand for *La Bataille* was tea dancing. I often went to spend a late afternoon at one of the large cafés near the Bois de Boulogne, as was the habit of many of the people I met in Paris.

On one afternoon I was attracted by the beauty of a girl of eighteen or so who was accompanied by a very dignified old lady—a French *grande dame*—who kept careful charge of her young companion. The girl was having considerable difficulty enjoying herself.

Finally the old lady found something which interested her more, and a little while later, at my request, an acquaintance brought the girl over to my table and introduced us. I asked the girl, whom I shall call Lucille, to dance. While we did, at her insistence, I discussed my career and the reason I was in Paris.

"But it appears I won't be here much longer," I said. "I'm having too much trouble at the studio. About the sets." I explained the producer's plans for filming the marine scenes of *La Bataille*.

"I don't know a thing about making motion pictures, Mr. Hayakawa," Lucille replied, "I just like to see them, but it seems to me you're right and he is wrong." She became pensive. As we moved about the dance floor her brow furrowed slightly and she appeared to be deep in thought.

"Is there something wrong?" I asked. "You seem so occupied. I hope my dancing with you won't get you in trouble with your companion."

Lucille shook her head and smiled. Then she suddenly asked, "Will you meet me for lunch tomorrow?"

"I'd be delighted."

"Good. Meet me, say, at noon, at the Café de la Paix."

"Alone?" I flashed a glance at her elderly companion who was now sitting impatiently watching us.

"My aunt is a fussbudget." Lucille raised her chin in mock defiance and laughed. "Don't worry about her. Just meet me."

I agreed to do so, and was about to ask just what it was she had in mind when the orchestra launched into a song from one of the current New York musical comedy successes. Lucille moved closer, pressing her warm, young body hard against mine. "Tell me, do you know Irene Castle? I wish I could dance the way she does," she said. We whirled around the floor. And as we did, I wondered just what it was this young lady had in mind for us to do after we finished lunch. I got the notion that dancing with me had slightly aroused her.

The next day, Lucille was waiting, sitting alone at a table on the sidewalk when I arrived at the Café de la Paix shortly before noon. She looked very appealing.

"How long is this mystery going to continue?" I asked when we had finished our lunch and the waiter had served coffee. Lucille smiled like the Mona Lisa and laughed softly.

"Now it's my secret and I'm having fun keeping it," she said. "Be patient, please."

We drank our coffee and I paid for the lunch. While I politely argued with our waiter about his tip and passed a few moments in good-natured banter, Lucille strolled to the curb in front of the café and waved. A few moments later a highly polished black Hispano-Suiza limousine drew up before her. The uniformed driver got out, stepped swiftly around the magnificent car, politely touched his cap and opened the rear door. He inclined his head deferentially when I walked up. We climbed in.

"Now where?" I inquired as Lucille and I settled back on the soft cushions and the car slowly moved away from the curb and into the traffic.

"He knows," she answered, pointing a gloved finger at the back of the chauffeur's neck.

"But I don't." I lighted a cigar and rolled the window nearest me down slightly to let the smoke escape.

"Heavens, Mr. Hayakawa!" Lucille exclaimed. "Don't you like just a little mystery? I would think that being from Japan——" She closed her eyes and relaxed her features. Looking at her, I once again got the feeling she wanted to be taken sexually. I wondered if we might be bound for a small hotel on the Left Bank for an hour of stolen rapture. She was young, but most mature. And physically attractive. Still, Lucille didn't really seem the type.

We drove along the Boulevard des Capucines, past the famed Madeleine, then turned and passed through the short street which leads from there into the Place de là Concorde.

Then we crossed one of the many bridges linking the right bank of the Seine with the left and came in sight of the Hôtel des Invalides, where Napoleon is entombed. The high golden dome of the great building flashed in the bright sunlight.

A minute or two later the car pulled up before a large ornate stone building prefaced by a short flight of wide steps. Uniformed guards flanked its center entry.

"I confess I find this all very strange," I said to Lucille as we left the car and climbed the steps to enter the building.

"I mean it to be," she said. She giggled. Then she asked, "Are you married, Mr. Hayakawa?"

"Yes, I am."

"Papa says I find married men too attractive."

I smiled and took her hand.

Lucille led me along a wide corridor in which, at intervals, guards in French naval uniform stood rigidly at attention. Each one we passed saluted and didn't return his rifle to rest position until our backs were to him.

"In here!" Lucille suddenly exclaimed. She tugged at my arm, directing me to a heavy oak door bearing a brass plate identifying the room behind it as the office of the Minister of the Marine. I opened it and we went inside, passed a receptionist-secretary who smiled recognition and bobbed her head at Lucille, and into an inner office.

As we entered, Lucille said, "Hello, Papa," to the trimly dressed gentleman sitting behind a large desk at the far end of the room. He rose and came forward to meet us. "This is my friend, Mr. Hayakawa, Papa." Lucille introduced us. We shook hands. "He is here from the United States to act in a motion picture about the naval battles of——" She looked at me.

"The Russo-Japanese War," I supplied, smiling.

"Yes," Lucille went on, her voice bubbling. "He needs more ships."

"So you said last night," her father remarked, looking at me.

I waited. I had absolutely no idea of what was going on or what I should say.

"Then see that he gets some!" Lucille blurted impatiently.

Her father ignored her and concentrated on me. He asked, "Is it true that you and the people at Vandal-Delac studios are planning to film *Croix de Fer*?" I said yes and recounted to him what I had told Lucille the previous afternoon. He snorted derisively and reached for the telephone behind him on his desk. Speaking rapidly, in French, he asked to be connected with the commander of the naval garrison at Toulon, on the southern coast.

"There is an American actor here to make a film on a naval theme," Lucille translated for me as her father spoke. "It will be in our interest to help him. . . . Vandal-Delac is producing the picture. . . . I know, but . . . Very well. . . . Hm? . . . Hayakawa. . . . Ha-ya-ka-wa. Oh? One moment, I'll ask him." The minister turned to me. "The commander wants to know if you are the one he saw in *The Cheat*."

"Yes, I am," I said, surprised.

"That picture was very popular over here," the minister said. He resumed his conversation with Toulon. "Yes, he says he is. Now, I want you to co-operate with Mr. Hayakawa as much as possible. . . . Good, good. . . . Sunday?" He again turned to me, asking, "Can you be in Toulon on Sunday?"

"Certainly," I said, "but——"

"Sunday will be fine," he said into the telephone. "Yes. . . . Yes. . . . Thank you. Goodbye." He hung up.

"If you and your people can be in Toulon on Sunday you can begin work on the marine scene immediately," he said. "I have requested the base commander there to give you complete co-operation."

I gaped at him. Ten minutes before he hadn't even seen my face. Now he was putting the French navy at my disposal. I was absolutely numb with surprise. Lucille squealed and threw her arms around her father's neck.

"Is it usually this way?" I asked. "I mean—ah, I don't know what to say." The minister shrugged and laughed. "I doubt if we will need the fleet for a war," he said. "You might as well use it for the film. Good luck, Mr. Hayakawa." He extended his hand. I shook it warmly and left his office feeling lightheaded.

That evening I told the president of Vandal-Delac and our director Violet what had taken place. After they recovered from their amazement, we made plans. When Saturday came, we took the eight o'clock evening express for Toulon. We arrived the following morning and reported to the commander of the naval base.

"We will need quite a bit for what we have in mind," I told him. "How many ships are available?"

"Twenty-seven," the commander answered, "including cruisers and heavy battleships."

I plunged. "Can we use them all?"

"All!" The officer nearly shot out of his chair. "The minister didn't say . . ."

"How many then?" I said.

"Using them all would leave us high and dry, you understand. We have to keep at least four ships on call." The commander pursed his lips in thought and was silent for a moment. *"D'accord,"* he said finally. "You can use twenty-three."

I will never forget the look that came into Violet's face when he realized we had twenty-three actual naval vessels to use in the picture. His expression was that of a small boy at Christmas.

After agreeing on a date to begin filming, we returned to Paris and began to pack our equipment and get ready to trek south. We took eleven cameras to Toulon, along with Russian naval uniforms, Japanese uniforms, lighting equipment and everything else judged necessary.

The picture got under way without a hitch. In the interest of operations I was permitted to wear the uniform of a
French naval captain (unless I was before the camera), so
I would have no difficulty commanding the French sailors
we used as bit players and extras. For crewmen on the
ships standing in for the Japanese fleet we brought in
Chinese from Marseilles. Overnight, the Toulon naval
base became a miniature Hollywood.

"This whole thing is unreal," Violet remarked to me as
we considered the bare fact that we were in charge of a
fair-sized segment of the French fleet. "Absolutely unreal."
He took his hat off and scratched his head. "What in god's
name did you do, Hayakawa—hypnotize the Minister of
the Marine?"

"I met his daughter at a tea dance."

"At a tea dance!" Violet roared until tears rolled down
his cheeks. "No one will ever believe it," he said when he
got control of himself. "At a tea dance." He again shook
with laughter and went off to check some equipment.

Recreating the famous battle, the Battle of Tsushima
Bay, in which most of the Russian fleet was sent to the
bottom, was the high point of *La Bataille*. It kindled old
memories. I remembered how wildly, with unbridled joy,
I had celebrated the great victory with my fellow students
at the Naval Preparatory School in Tokyo.

Early on the morning of the first day we spent shooting
the scene, the ships selected to represent the Japanese fleet
commanded by my idol Admiral Togo wheeled into the
clasic T-attack formation off the rocky coast of Toulon.
Crowds lined the shore to watch. As the officer, I paced the
bridge of the second ship in the formation, a cruiser. At
Violet's signal I gave the command to fire. The guns
opened up. The first salvo split the cool morning air with
a thunderous roar. The concussion knocked our camera-

man flat on his back. The camera collapsed on top of him. We had to stop all action, reform our position and reshoot after detailing a group of sailors to hold the cameraman and his equipment in place. Dazed, but game, he plugged his ears and went back to work.

We shot naval battle sequences for close to three weeks. Then we returned to the studio in Paris to film the interior scenes and complete the picture.

When *La Bataille* was released it erupted into an international success. The film played for two years in Paris alone. In the United States it was distributed under the title, *The Danger Line.*

La Bataille also was shown in Japan. There the great Admiral Togo, himself, went to see it.

There is a scene in *La Bataille* in which, as Admiral Togo did following the Battle of Tsushima Bay, I stand fighting to control my emotions, and pay tribute to the gallant Japanese sailors who die in the battle. When I acted that scene I tried to think as I felt he must have thought. I spoke as I believed he must have spoken—out of his heart.

The admiral, taken back to that moment in May, 1905, and once again experiencing the emotion he felt then, cried.

So once again my early naval training helped me to perfect a role as it had when I played the young naval lieutenant in *Hototogisu* at the Japanese Theatre in Los Angeles. But this time I had played the part of a lieutenant of the admiral who was the idol of my boyhood and youth —Togo, the man for whom I had been willing to die by my own hand. Thus, in a way, I did become an admiral and achieve my father's ambition for me after all, if only for a few hours.

The tremendous success of *La Bataille* brought me an offer to play at the fashionable Casino de Paris, in Paris. I did so in a French-English vaudeville sketch and became

quite popular with the nightclub crowd. I had improved
my French by then; and being partially on vacation, I
began to work on a novel. I called it *The Bandit Prince*.
It was published in English, in the United States, in 1926,
the year I returned from France. Afterward I dramatized
the story as a forty-minute sketch and played in it in vaudeville at the Palace Th atre in New York, and on tour
throughout the Unit d States and Canada.

I was appearing at the Casino de Paris when a delegation
of theatrical notables from London called on me with an
invitation to take part in, a cording to the formally lettered
scroll they presented, a

> Royal Performance in the presence of Their
> Majesties The King & Queen on Thursday,
> December 13th 1923, at the London Coli-
> seum.

The performance was to be held for the financial benefit
of the British Variety Artistes' Benevolent Fund and Insti-
tution, and would consist of six parts. My appearance was
to be the climax of the entertainment.

"Sir William Archer has written a play perfectly suited
to your abilities and person, Mr. Hayakawa," I was informed by the producer Maurice Volny. "It is titled *The
Samurai*. May we tell London you will participate?"

I fully appreciated the honor, but I had to say, "I am
playing here in Paris. You mean for me to drop everything and . . ."

Mr. Volny turned a little pale. "But you must play!
My God! You can't insult the King and Queen!"

I certainly had no intention of insulting the King of
England, I assured him. "But," I said, "I have an obligation to fulfill here. I just can't drop what I'm doing. I'm
under contract."

"This is all a tempest in a teapot," one of Volny's companions observed. He turned to me. "If you can take time to play for that evening, I'm sure an arrangement can be made by which you can rehearse *The Samurai* here in Paris."

"If that can be done I will be honored to take part in the performance," I told them.

The necessary arrangement was made. Maurice Volny saw to it that the other members of the cast, Lewis Gilbert, Ann Trevor and Dora De Winton, joined me in Paris for rehearsals and staging. We prepared during the day, while I continued with my performances at the Casino de Paris at night. Then, shortly before the night of the Royal Performance in London, we all went there for final dress rehearsal on the Coliseum stage. I met the author of the play, Sir William Archer, at that time. He was mainly a dramatic critic. He was a stanch supporter of Ibsen and realistic drama and a great friend of George Bernard Shaw. But as a playwright himself, he seems to have favored exotic themes, for he authored at least two improbable melodramas, *The Samurai* and *The Green Goddess*. Both involved a clash between East and West. In *The Green Goddess* the former was represented by a principal character who was an Oxford-educated Indian raja. In *The Samurai* the East was presented in the character of the son of a proud Japanese samurai family. This, of course, was my role in the play.

Following the Command Performance a party was given for the participants by the present Duke of Windsor, who was then the Prince of Wales and heir apparent to the throne. The party brought me in contact with British high society for the first time. It was quite formal. The Prince made a speech congratulating us all, and I was called upon to respond.

"While you are alive," I said, "you must spend your life

pleasantly. We have to be optimists. It's too bad there are so many pessimists in this world. Take the doughnut. An optimist looks and sees the ring, but the pessimist only sees the hole."

All things considered, I thought this would strike the English as funny. But everyone looked strange. I thought first that they didn't understand my humor, but later I learned that English doughnuts have no holes. My speech was a complete failure. I sat down in chagrin at my mistake. I felt like a fool, and I'm sure the Prince of Wales thought me one along with everyone else. Since that time I have thought twice before indulging in comedy. Not that I don't enjoy telling or hearing a good funny remark or story. It's just that there is nothing so devastating to the ego as the embarrassed silence that follows when a joke flops. Especially in English society. The English have the knack of making a person who commits such an error feel wretched.

The interest of the English public in *The Samurai* after I performed in it before the King and Queen was so great and demanding that the producers convinced me I should take the play on tour. To allow this, they made a financial settlement with the Casino de Paris and the French producers who had planned to present me in a play in Paris. But first, we took the play to Paris.

Then we went to Liverpool. It was in Liverpool that I found myself in the disquieting position of being cautiously, almost innocently, stalked by a very charming, very wonderful young girl. She was playing opposite me in *The Samurai*, and had done so since the play was first presented.

I had a large suite in the hotel in Liverpool, and I asked her to have dinner with me one night following a performance. Having dinner together in my suite became a habit. One Sunday, she came and remained with me quite late.

It was pouring rain outside and she was reluctant to leave in the storm. I sent down for a bottle of wine, and after the waiter had left, feeling things were approaching a head, I asked her: "Do you want to go home in this weather or do you want to stay?"

At this, she blushed red as a lobster. I looked at her expectantly, but she refused to answer my question. But because she blushed I got her coat. "Perhaps you had better go," I said.

She half nodded and I put her coat over her shoulders. Then, suddenly gripped by an intense desire to have her, I took back the coat, put my hands on her shoulders, and turned her to face me. She refused to look up into my face, so I kidded her, remarking: "I guess I'm not hot enough for you. You must be cold. Come near the fire."

I drew her to her feet and guided her to the fireplace. We sat down and stared into the flames for perhaps a half hour without touching one another or speaking. It was a curious experience. A very strange one. I could have taken her—as much as I might wish—but even when the body lusts and the mind is slave to the sexual desire, something of the conscience remains. The moral sense intervenes. I was restrained by the knowledge that I had no right to have her. This has happened more than once. Seduction has come very close. But when the last and final moment of decision has come, desire has left me. Both my mind and body have become numb—cold, and devoid of the necessary passion. It has happened that even if I wanted to take the woman, I could not.

There is something of Zen influence in this. Not that to follow the way of Zen is to be celibate. It is true that those who give themselves entirely to Zen, the disciples who become monks, must put sexual passion and desire to sleep forever. It is part of demanded discipline. But the lay disciple, he who is married, is not so restrained. In Zen, however, to abandon oneself to sexual desire is to degrade oneself. Those who would be monks are told this. The layman is left to go the middle path according to his conscience as developed through Zen practice. And practice exacts a morality which refuses to allow transgression. The Zen mind rebels. It foresees the consequences—the suffering which will be produced by the pleasure of a few moments.

It restrained me. I replaced the coat on her shoulders and sent her back to her hotel.

The young actress and I remained just good friends. Better friends, I believe, than we would have been had I seduced her. Our moment came and passed unstolen. The opportunity and desire did not come again. The tour of *The Samurai* ran its course and came to an end. We parted professional company, and I quite forgot about her. However, I stayed on in England to make two films, *The Illustrious Prince* and one the name of which I cannot recall. And when I left London by train to catch the channel steamer back to France, a large bouquet of flowers was delivered to my compartment with a note from the girl telling me goodbye and wishing me good luck.

The Illustrious Prince was a contemporary setting film about a Japanese prince visiting England incognito. I had a pleasant time making it. For one thing the British method contrasted greatly with all I was used to in Hollywood. There was little of the rough and tumble informality present at the studios in London. Rather, everything was quite formal. I found myself being invited to appear on the set to perform in a scene, and invited—each afternoon at three-thirty—to relax and take tea.

In all, I stayed in England about a year. Then I returned to Paris to film *J'ai Tué* and resume my vaudeville act at the Casino de Paris.

This activity soon palled, however, and when the picture

was completed, Tsuru and I took a vacation, touring as far north as Norway, as far south and east as Greece. Then we settled in Monte Carlo for a few weeks. There I caught the gambling fever. We were staying in a hotel in Nice, but every night found me at the tables in the Monte Carlo Casino. For a time my winnings balanced my losses and playing was nothing more than innocent diversion. But then I took up baccarat, at a very exclusive club, The Sporting Club. I played for fairly low stakes at first, but as the game began to intrigue me my bets increased. Thousands of dollars began to change hands at the flip of a card.

One evening I sat down to play against the Duke of Westminster; Citroen, the French automobile millionaire; a pair of wealthy Greeks who actually allowed themselves a gambling budget of $200,000 a season; and a South American known then as the Coffee King.

Westminster, as the duke was referred to, was reportedly worth millions, and was said to own half of London. He was an inveterate gambler, and a shrewd one. He played as if his life depended upon his winning. He was not particularly friendly or polite, and I did not like him. As we played he sat across the table looking like a statue. He moved little and spoke less. He angered me, and I gambled with him in defiance. I wanted to beat him, but the cards all fell his way. The game progressed and the stakes mounted to figures almost beyond belief. We six looked like characters in a melodrama, each one of us sitting silent, intent on our cards, immune to the excitement of the spectators who quickly gathered when word of our bets got around the casino. My experience with poker in Hollywood provided me with a straight face. I lost steadily, but my lack of expression concealed I was losing.

Finally I had enough. I withdrew from the game. When my losses were totaled, they came to 5,000,000 francs (about $965,000). It surprised everyone but me. My lack **of a show** of emotion had convinced those watching that I was winning, not losing.

The Casino paid Westminster, but he had won every franc I lost. I in turn paid the Casino.

Five million francs lost in one sitting is more than enough. I made a gesture of buying a round of champagne, said goodnight, and drove back to the hotel in Nice. I went to bed at 2:00 A.M., after telling the room clerk not to wake me before noon the next day.

However, the telephone in my room rang me awake early. "I told you not to wake me before twelve o'clock!" I barked sleepily into the handset.

The operator apologized profusely and then announced the Japanese Embassy in Paris was on the line. "Urgent," she said, connecting me.

"Yes?" I said.

"Mr. Hayakawa?"

"Yes. What is it?"

"Are you really Mr. Sessue Hayakawa?"

"Yes."

There was a long sigh at the Paris end of the wire. I was on the verge of hanging up when I was suddenly asked: "Aren't you dead?"

"What do you mean 'dead'? Don't joke. It's too early."

"The morning papers here report you committed suicide last night. They say you lost five million francs gambling. Did you?"

"Yes, I did," I said.

"They say that because you were unhappy about the loss you jumped off a cliff."

"Obviously, I did not. The papers are full of nonsense. I am here in Nice," I said, emphasizing each word; "and, if you must know, I am in bed. Kindly call the papers and tell them so."

"It's strange, but you are really alive?"

"Yes," I said, and losing my patience I hung up and went back to sleep.

The whole affair smacks of the ridiculous now, but was treated with dead seriousness then. Later that day I was told that another Japanese, from Italy, had gambled his fortune away at the casino while I was battling with West-minster. Then he had written a letter in Japanese, stuffed it into his coat pocket, and jumped off one of the high cliffs surrounding Monte Carlo. The body was so bruised and battered it couldn't be recognized, and when the letter in Japanese was found the immediate conclusion was that I had been driven to suicide by my loss. The news spread like spilled water. The newspapers eventually corrected their mistake, but for years afterward I would run into people who had only heard the first story. They invariably registered surprise and incredulously asked, "Are you still living?"

Even the noted *New York Times*, widely recognized for accuracy, was some months late in reporting: "A Paris report that Sessue Hayakawa, the Japanese actor, had committed suicide in Monte Carlo, was disclosed yesterday to be without foundation. Mr. Hayakawa is playing here in vaudeville." This item appeared in the *Times* on March 6, 1927, more than eighteen months after I had returned to New York from France, and almost a year after I had starred in a play, *The Love City*, for Lee Shubert.

To play in *The Love City* was the reason I had returned to the United States after nearly three years in France and England. Shortly after returning to Paris from Monte Carlo, I had met Lee Shubert one evening while I was nightclubbing with some friends. He had just seen the play in Berlin, where *The Love City* was originally produced, and when he saw me he decided to acquire the American rights and produce it in New York. His offer of the leading role brought me back to the United States. Otherwise, I think I would have remained in Paris.

The Love City, written by Hans Bachwitz and staged by Stuart Walker, opened at the Little Theatre, on Forty-fourth Street, in New York, on January 25, 1926, after out-of-town tryouts which included performances in Scranton and Wilkes-Barre, Pa. I played the part of Chang Lo, a Chinese dealing in women and opium, whose greed and despotism ultimately brings him death at the hands of a wife-deserting Englishman, who was played by Earle Larimore. A protégé of David Belasco, Catherine Dale Owen, performed the role of the prize in Chang Lo's band of prostitutes. The play is an allegory of soul and body and passion and love, and the second act consists of a dream sequence in which all three of us took other parts.

Opening night was a big event. I was billed as appearing in my first Broadway play. Professional friends including actress Helen MacKellar, the famous Alla Nazimova and Ben Lyon, who has won enduring fame in England, attended and came backstage to wish me well.

The play got good reviews and ran for some months, first at the Little Theatre and then at the Klaw Theatre on Forty-fifth Street, before moving on to Chicago. Appearing in it was a most rewarding experience.

While I was in *The Love City* I was invited to take part in the Forty-fourth Actor's Fund Annual Benefit. It was held at Jolson's Theatre the evening of February 2, 1926, at which time I had the pleasure of performing on a program which included E. H. Sothern, Laurette Taylor, Blanche Ring, Otto Kruger, Grant Mitchell and the wonderful vaudeville team of Van and Schenck. We were directed by Daniel Frohman.

Life moved very quickly after I returned to New York. The play kept me busy, and after the play came vaudeville.

The Keith people asked me to play the Palace and tour their circuit in a forty minute dramatization of my novel, *The Bandit Prince*. In spite of the motion pictures, which eventually killed it, vaudeville was still very popular in the late 1920's.

I was in vaudeville when I decided to settle in the New York area. Tsuru and I had lived out of suitcases and trunks in hotels ever since we left Hollywood. Being rootless, so to speak, had begun to irritate us both.

So I purchased the rambling English Tudor brick and slate-roofed mansion I still own on Long Island. It is in Great Neck, and when I bought it in June, 1927, for $45,000, the front windows commanded an enchanting view of the bay which opens on the west end of Long Island Sound. One of the reasons I acquired the house was the Soundview Golf Course, which was right next door.

My vaudeville sketch was quite successful. The *Times* graciously reported that my part of Chang, the bandit prince, was "as excellently tailored a role for Hayakawa as could be found anywhere." Such was the virtue of being the author. I made the character as singular as possible. Chang, the bandit prince, called the Manchurian Eagle, was a graduate of Harvard University who had veneered himself with the dash and habit of a Parisian *boulevardier*. Up to the minute in his thinking and professional method, he carried on his illegal and nefarious operations in a dramatically modern—quite modern for that time—way. He used an airplane.

I performed *The Bandit Prince* in vaudeville throughout 1926 and 1927. Then, in 1928, I appeared in a more serious sketch, *The Man Who Laughed*, by Edgar Allan Wolf. My leading lady in it was Lucille Lortel, a bright, engaging ingenue, who went on to bigger and better things. She now owns and operates the Theatre de Lys in New York's Greenwich Village, the renowned off-Broadway playhouse where *The Threepenny Opera* has been playing to packed houses since 1955.

The Bandit Prince was the more popular of the two sketches. It entertained audiences with more action and thrills. But after two years, a change was indicated. Anyway, *The Man Who Laughed* contained more drama. It gave me a better opportunity to display depth and perception in my acting. Taking the stage as the Manchurian Eagle meant dash and swagger.

It was in 1927, too, while I was busy in vaudeville, that I took steps to bring Zen to others. I leased an apartment on New York's upper west side and had it converted into a temple and Zen study hall. There I provided leadership for a small group of Zen students, both Oriental and Occidental. Americans at that time were becoming aware of Zen Buddhism through the writing of Zen master and scholar D. T. Suzuki, who is now recognized and esteemed as Zen's foremost spokesman in the West.

The group I formed met weekly to study and practice together in the ancient communal ways which characterize those who choose the way of Zen and the rigid, formal instruction peculiar to the monastic community. Assisting me, I had a Zen Buddhist priest named Sasaki. Together we sought to bring Zen knowledge to others who wished to find themselves and a measure of peace through its teachings. We were successful in building a serious devoted group. The temple flourished for some years. But when my professional activities took me far afield from New York and Sasaki married and returned to Japan, its activity became dormant.

The years spent in New York and on tour in vaudeville passed as does the sand in an hourglass. They did so for many people. The closing years of the 1920's, from 1926 through the collapse of the stock market in 1929, were strange and wonderful years made up of days in which tomorrows never figured. Everyone appeared to be living for the moment, and for the moment only. Stocks skyrocketed. Money was plentiful. Existence moved quickly, unchecked. There was a wildness and abandon in the way people conducted themselves. They lived hard, played hard, and drank hard. Desires ruled. Nobody seemed to worry. Life was too much fun.

I moved along in the sweep of that life—with it, yet apart —part of the panorama but not of the almost sensual embrace which characterized living then. Zen remained my balance wheel.

The United States and the ways of her people have always fascinated and impressed me. So has the way of life in France, where the verve and pace is much the same. People are very much alive in the United States, but only in an earthbound sense. They cling too much to elusive values. Thus, conversely, to the fully enlightened disciple of Zen, they are as if dead. They move in a world of illusion.

I have often been asked why, if I believe in Zen, have I so indulged myself with all that is ephemeral in human being, with all that is materialistic and peculiar to the hedonist.

The answer is simple. Although I have found a true salvation in Zen, I do not consider myself ascetic in the monastic sense. Zen does not demand the hair shirt and the begging bowl. After all, to move in Zen is to live with life, not apart from it, or in opposition to its flow. I have a taste for the finer things, and since my profession has abundantly rewarded me, I have catered to my tastes. I see nothing wrong in this; there is only wrongness in attaching too much importance to the ephemeral, all that cannot and does not last. All that is of human existence is ephemeral, though it last a thousand thousand years. The tighter it is grasped, the tighter the ego seeks to confine it to possession and indulges in selfish hedonism, the faster all drains away. Consider how short a time water can be cupped in the hands.

Life as it is known by man, the atmosphere which marks his civilizations, is pleasant if let be, taken unto itself as a phase, but not as the ultimate. That is why, in the environment in which destiny placed me, I took up playing such games as poker and golf and delighted in all the symbols of success prevalent in western civilization. Conditions demanded that I do so. Not being a saint or hypocrite, but a man and fallible, I have partaken, but not with the attitude of the materialist and the hedonist. My attitude is rather difficult to explain. I cannot communicate the root of how I feel, but I can say the tangible indications of what it might be, how I might feel, are not indications at all. I am detached through Zen.

Tsuru and I were married fifteen years when our first child, a son, was born in New York City in 1929. He is named Yukio.

I was still performing in vaudeville when Yukio was born. I continued to appear at the Palace Theatre in New York City and to tour until the fall of 1931, when David Belasco, the famous playwright and producer, asked me to appear in a play called *The Honorable Mr. Wong.*

David Belasco was truly the grand old man of the American stage when we met. He was seventy-eight years old. He was wearing a black suit when we first faced each other. White, heavily starched French cuffs protruded from the sleeves of his coat, accentuating his expressive hands. Above the clerical collar that was his eccentric mark of character his somewhat heavy head, capped with an unkempt, flowing white mane, was a fascinating study. I found his eyes—the depths of them—to be as spellbinding as his conversation.

"I know Cecil very well," he casually remarked when I recalled working for Mr. De Mille in *The Cheat*; "his brother William, too, of course. And their father. Cecil, you know, assisted me with the writing of *The Return of Peter Grimm*. He is always busy. Not in a rush, but busy. Thorough.

"Well, now!" he abruptly shifted. *"The Honorable Mr. Wong."* He settled back in his chair and began to outline the play for me.

It was difficult to realize later that when he and I first discussed the play David Belasco was a dying man, and that he would die the next May. He was so interesting and interested when he talked. He did not look or act his age. I believe the demands of his work, his love for it, didn't allow him any time to feel old. However, *The Honorable Mr. Wong* did not get beyond the planning stage of production. I had just received a copy of the script and was about to begin rehearsing when Belasco died.

I very much regret that death denied me the opportunity to act for David Belasco. It would have been a privilege to do so. I'm sure *The Honorable Mr. Wong* would have been an excellent and successful production.

Belasco favored dramas on Oriental themes. He, himself, wrote and produced a dramatization of John Luther Long's story, *Madame Butterfly*. It was from Belasco's play that Puccini took his famous opera.

Belasco also wrote (with John Luther Long), produced and directed *The Darling of the Gods*, a drama of heroism, patriotism and love, based on an obscure incident in Japanese history—an unsuccessful rebellion staged in 1868.

Cecil B. De Mille once planned to produce *The Darling of the Gods* as a motion picture, and went to great expense acquiring and importing lavish Japanese costumes and properties for it. Some of the latter, weapons in particular, were of the highest historical significance, having been the property of the great Tokugawa family which rose to ruling power in Japan early in the seventeenth century. Mr. De Mille showed me some of the Tokugawa weapons when I was with Paramount, and put into my hands one of the finest samurai swords I ever saw. The edge of the blade was so keen I placed a piece of rice paper between my lips, holding it so that it covered my nose, and held my breath because even a warm exhalation would have destroyed the sharpness of the sword's edge. Unfortunately, the film was never made.

David Belasco's death, in May, 1931, halted all plans and expectations for my reappearance on a Broadway stage in a full-length play. I did, however, acquire the right to produce *The Honorable Mr. Wong* in Japan. I had the script translated.

The idea of doing a play had, of course, lessened my interest in vaudeville; and even though there was no chance of doing the play now, I did not want to continue in variety entertainment. I was tired of vaudeville, and vaudeville itself was tired and dying. The tremendous success of silent films had slowly made the public apathetic to the once great medium. And now, in 1931, with sound films to entertain it, the public was generally weary of variety.

So, interested in producing *The Honorable Mr. Wong* in Japan, I leased my home in Great Neck, and with Tsuru and young Yukio returned to my homeland. I went back an extremely rich man, on whom fortune had smiled long and bright during the twenty-two years that had passed since I first sailed aboard the *Aki-maru* for San Francisco.

Upon arriving in Tokyo I lost little time getting settled with my small family in a comfortable house in the suburbs and proceeding to re-establish myself in Japanese life and to integrate into the modern phase of theatre. With myself in the title role, I produced *The Honorable Mr. Wong*

at Tokyo's Imperial Theatre. The play was an immediate
success. It enjoyed a long and profitable run in Tokyo,
after which I played in it on tour off and on for the next
five years.

In addition to the play, I was kept busy making films.
My great success in American and French motion pictures
had made me a box office "draw" that Japanese film producers eagerly sought to capitalize upon. There was no
lack of work. However, I made a point of limiting my
professional activities, lest I nullify my popularity by doing
too much. Even so, I was busy. And I was not beyond the
vision of Hollywood. I was called back there for a short
time in 1933. By then Famous Players-Lasky had become
Paramount Studios, and Paramount convinced me to
return and make my first American film since *The Vermilion Pencil* in 1922. The picture was my first in sound,
Daughter of the Dragon, a mystery. I appeared in it with
Anna May Wong and Warner Oland. He was not an
Oriental—I believe he was of Swedish descent—but he performed Far Eastern character roles extremely well. He is
best remembered for his creation of the Chinese detective
Charlie Chan on the screen.

My role in *Daughter of the Dragon* was that of an Ameri-
can-born Chinese, a police detective. I enjoyed it very
much. For once, I was not the villain. I have played the
villain too many times, I think, even though I did play
romantic roles in my early films. Sometime, just for once,
I would like to play the hero.

Following completion of this film I returned to Japan
and resumed my production of *The Honorable Mr. Wong.*
And in 1934 I appeared in the role of Claudius in a production of Shakespeare's *Hamlet* presented at the Meiji
Theatre in Tokyo under the auspices of the Tsubouchi
Memorial Theatre Museum of Waseda University. The
title role was taken by an actress, Yaeko Mizutani.

Except for playing in *The Honorable Mr. Wong,*
Hamlet and a few Japanese films, my years in Japan during
the 1930's were uncomplicated peaceful ones in comparison
to the busy decade I passed in Hollywood following my
graduation from the University of Chicago. Simplicity is
a tradition in Japan, and I fell under its influence when I
returned. I suddenly belonged more to myself and my
family. And my family was increasing. My first daughter,
Yoshiko, was born in Tokyo in 1936; and her sister Fujiko,
two years later.

But by the time Fujiko was born, I was again gone from
Japan. In 1937, Pathé Studios in Paris sent me an offer to
appear in the film, *Yoshiwara.* I accepted, and packed my
suitcases for what I expected would be a stay of perhaps
three months. The events of the world, however, were
shaping against me to alter the course of my destiny beyond
all expectation. The fateful storm clouds of World War II
were slowly gathering over Europe. The militarists of
Japan, then at war with China, were plotting, even then,
moves which would plunge my country into global conflict.
The effect upon me would be an enforced exile in France
for twelve years.

9   An Oasis in the Desert

ON ARRIVING IN PARIS I ONCE AGAIN FELL WILLING PREY
to the magic and charm of that beautiful city. A decade had
passed since I last had been there, but it did not seem that
Paris had changed. Although the rumors of war were
gathering strength by the day, life in the City of Light was
as bustling as ever. The rumble of conflict was still in the
distance. There was considerable optimism abroad. But
then, optimism is peculiar to national thought immediately preceding a war. Few persons ever truly wish for war.
Instead most thoughts are directed toward staving it off,
even though all signs point to its coming.

The French film studios were extremely active when I
reported to begin work on *Yoshiwara*. Every film company
had a full schedule of productions laid out. Plans for the
future were being drafted. If war was to come, it would
come. In the meantime the feeling was for creating. There
was plenty of work to be done.

The French producers were glad to have me back in Paris. For when I completed *Yoshiwara*, I received many other offers. Although more than ten years had passed since I had made *La Bataille* and *J'ai Tué*, I was remembered with favor and appreciation. The opportunities presented demanded I stay for a while. Therefore, I put aside my intention to return to Japan and remained in Paris to make a number of pictures for Pathé and for the Gaumont company.

My second picture was *The Cheat (La Forfaiture)* with Louis Jouvet and Victor Francen. Until we started work on *The Cheat* Jouvet and I had never met. I had heard a great deal about him, however, and he lived up to his notices.

Louis Jouvet had a strong personality, I found. Erich Von Stroheim, whose films were the rage of Hollywood about the time I left there, was now in France. He had made a film, *L'Alibi*, with Jouvet the previous year. Von Stroheim, as self-confident a man and artist as ever made a motion picture, admitted he literally shook in his shoes when he first appeared on the set to play a scene with Jouvet. The aura of the Frenchman's greatness was that compelling, he said.

My initial experience with Jouvet, however, was considerably different. He portrayed my secretary in the picture, and on our first day together at the studio we rehearsed a scene in which he brought me a letter. I seated myself at the desk on the set and after a moment Jouvet entered and came toward me to hand me the letter. I looked up and into his eyes. He handed me the letter and then turned and left the set. I waited, thinking he had gone on some short errand. But he didn't return for nearly an hour. And when he did reappear, he told our director, "I'm sorry. I have worked on stage with a lot of people, but I've never had stage fright like I have today. You'll have to excuse me. Victor [Francen] suggested a drink to quiet my nerves. So I've been with him, drinking champagne."

I heard about this curious development later, and I asked Jouvet why he had stage fright.

"I just can't watch your eyes!" he exclaimed.

"My eyes!" His explanation puzzled me. "Why my eyes?" I said. "I don't glare at you in this scene. All I do is . . ."

"I know, I know," he admitted. "But there is something in your eyes. Something that makes other people afraid of you. I just can't stand to look into them."

"But this is absurd," I laughed. I was embarrassed. "Please don't let it trouble you."

It took some doing, but I finally convinced Jouvet not to take the disquieting expression he found in my eyes seriously. After that we got along very well, for acting with him was far from difficult. He possessed a deep understanding, infinite patience, and an 'most occult insight into the demands of a role.

Louis Jouvet, I think, was a shining example of the truly great artist in my profession. Only small men whose egos dominate them completely make others unsure of themselves and prone to worry and trepidation stemming from anxiety. That is why, I believe, when one meets a truly great actor or actress—one who is obviously above the pettiness which so often characterizes so many in the theatre and in motion pictures, the reaction is one of, "Why, he's human! He's just like the rest of us!" And rightly so. An actor cannot allow his ego to push him up and out of touch with the very fountain of his professional ability—life itself.

The film Jouvet and I played in together was quite successful. So much so, that like this original American picture remade in France, *The Cheat* was made into a play; and I was signed to re-create my movie role on the stage.

The part I played called for me to inflict considerable physical abuse upon the female lead who, incidentally, was the mistress of the producer. One day at rehearsal I grabbed her by the hair, according to the director's orders, and threw her to the stage. The scene was hardly over when the producer stomped on stage and protested my violence. "In the movie you do it just once," he said, "but I don't want you doing it to her every night on stage. We'll have to work something else out."

"I'm not hurting her," I said. "Not in the slightest. It only seems that I am."

He shook his head in doubt. "I don't think it's necessary, this violence. It's not good to hurt anybody physically, whatever the demands of the script."

"A little physical discomfort can be beneficial," I rejoined. "Physical pain has the power to tighten our minds —make us alert. For example, many times, dancers are slapped with rulers. Singers, too. Their minds become scattered. But at the moment a little physical pain is inflicted the mind becomes organized and alert. Punishment is motivated from two sources, hatred and love. A teacher will punish a student to make that student a better person, to tighten the mind.

"You love the girl too much," I told the producer. "You're letting your emotions blind you to what is necessary."

"Perhaps I am." He smiled. "Just the same I'm not interested in having her come off stage every night black and blue."

"Once she concentrates on what is happening, I doubt if she'll be hurt very much. Her mind will see to that. But it must be tightened," I emphasized. "And in order to do it she must have an incentive. If you expect her to react according to the script I've got to throw her down. Physical pain will produce the fastest incentive. It is most effective. Are you familiar with Zen?" I asked.

"I've heard about it. I understand you're quite an

authority. But what has Zen got to with your tossing the young lady around?"

"A Zen priest, a teacher, when he is instructing a disciple and asks a question, will say, 'Answer quick! Or thirty blows for you!' And he will hit the student if he is unable to focus on concentrated thought. It has been proven that pain can lead to enlightenment and the right road to salvation. You see, when there is pain, the moment you feel it, nothingness comes. The stimulation of pain clears worldly thought away. Zen involves discipline of the mind so as to deny the body. In Zen, the moment you feel pain, on the basis of previous learning and experience, you are able to find truth. It's the same with any art.

"Now," I went on, "It may seem cruel to you when I hurt the woman you love, but through the physical and mental pain I inflict she is able to produce what her art demands. She will develop an insight far greater than any she could hope to foster logically by intellectualizing what her part demands.

"Let me tell you a story—a *koan* it is called in Zen. One of the great Zen masters of old, Gutei, made a habit out of extending an index finger whenever a disciple asked him a question about Zen. Time came when a young follower took to imitating Gutei. When the master extended an index finger, the disciple, surreptitiously, of course, also extended an index finger. The result was the other disciples laughed.

"Came a time, however, when Gutei caught his mimic. Without a word the master took out a knife, took the young disciple's hand, cut off the offending finger and threw it away. The maimed pupil went off howling in pain.

" 'Halt!' Gutei shouted to him. The disciple stopped and looked back. Gutei extended his index finger. Without realizing it was no longer part of him, the disciple

raised his. Then, suddenly, a beatific smile spread across
his tear-stained face. He was enlightened."

The producer listened very intently while I told this
story. And when I finished, he nodded and said, *"D'accord.*
I understand now. Do it your way." After that we had no
trouble achieving the effect desired of the scene.

Late in 1938, the Demofilm company approached me to
make a picture called *Macao, L'Enfer Du Jeu* (Macao,
The Gambling Hell), and gave me a chance to participate in
its production, both financially and artistically.

Macao, as the film was billed simply, out of the more
than one hundred and thirty films I have made in Hollywood, France, England and Japan, has a production history
which sets it apart from all my pictures except, perhaps,
The Bridge on the River Kwai.

Made from Roger Vitrac's screenplay of a novel by
Maurice Dekobra, and directed by Jean Delannoy, *Macao*
is an adventure story of high dramatic impact. The setting
is the infamous city which gave the film its title, Macao,
the seaport and gambling center near Hong Kong. Controlled by Portugal, Macao is an international port open
to traffic in all sorts of trade, illegal as well as legal. The
very setting of the picture indicates the type of story it
presents.

But the curious history of this picture hinges little on its
subject. It turns, rather, on the role my co-star played, and
particularly on the fact that he appeared in the picture.

My co-star in *Macao* was Erich Von Stroheim, throughout his entire professional life as a motion picture director
and actor the most colorful and controversial figure ever to
be associated with films. As an actor he was "The Man
You Love to Hate" to audiences which delighted in hissing
him when he appeared on the screen in the roles of impec-

cably uniformed Austrian and German army officers who were both cruel and sadistic, awesomely arrogant, and stiffly correct in military bearing and manner. As a director he was by turns a genius, then a spendthrift of unbelievably exorbitant proportions, and finally a taboo to all the studio heads in Hollywood, where he first won fame.

Von entered films in Hollywood shortly before I did. I first met him then, not long after he got his start playing six different Negro parts in D. W. Griffith's *The Birth of a Nation*. He learned motion picture production from Griffith, who also imparted to Von his lack of regard for expense. Griffith didn't care how much it cost to make a film, just so the result was what he desired. Von followed the same philosophy. It worked in the beginning. He worked his way up to become a director in 1918, and in the early 1920's his films were outshining all others in brilliance. You might say he made nothing but master-pieces. But the films he made were costly ones. And though his first ones made money, the ones he produced as his prestige and fame increased came to cost so much he priced himself right out of Hollywood. This and his sense of "I" and his insistence on absolute responsibility and direction, alienated studio after studio. He was hailed as a genius, but genuine hatred and fear of him forced him out of Hollywood after he was restricted from directing and demoted to the status of writer, a good status for many, but intolerable to him. He found new fame in French films, however, particularly in *La Grand Illusion*, in which his part, that of von Rauffenstein, the commandant of a German prisoner of war camp during World War I, was conceived by himself.

Von Stroheim never learned how to act. He learned from life itself, and was therefore highly subjective in his artistry, both as an actor and a director. Although he did not like to take advice, he did not consider himself omnipotent. He was a hard taskmaster and a perfectionist. But anyone who ever worked with him on a picture adored him. He looked forbidding and could act forbidding, but he was not irascible, mean or wantonly demanding. I liked him. We were similar in numerous ways as actors, and we worked well together. We never quarreled. And when we appeared together in *Macao*, we frequently dined and relaxed together.

Von Stroheim himself once admitted he could not talk for very long on the set, in any of the three or more languages he spoke, without swearing. Thus, when I reported to the Demofilm studios to begin *Macao*, and we confronted one another for the first time in years, that distinctive barely guttural voice of his rang out in greeting, "Sessue Hayakawa! You son of a bitch! I heard you were in town!" He fell silent for a moment, and then added, softly, "So here we are, you the inscrutable Oriental, I the crisp uniformed Prussian." He laughed heartily and slapped me on the back.

Macao was the only picture Von Stroheim and I appeared in together. His performance as Werner Krall, the crisp Prussian type, but a sympathetic role nonetheless, was one of his best. He gave the character touches of humanity Hollywood once loudly cried he did not have, on the screen or off.

The film was shot in Paris and in Nice and the waters near it which became the harbor of Macao for Krall's magnificent yacht. A number of scenes took place on the yacht, which was destroyed by an explosion at the close of the picture.

While we were filming in Nice, I once again crossed paths with a fortuneteller, a decrepit, stumbling old woman who loitered on the main street near our hotel and offered predictions to all who would stop to listen. Von and I

were on our way back to the hotel from dinner one evening
when we decided to learn what she had to say about us.
She peered closely at me, and though I was approaching
my fiftieth birthday, called me "young man." This greatly
amused Von Stroheim, who was two years older than
myself.

"Young man," she said, "you have great hope. Something you are making, working upon very hard, have
finished, perhaps, means a lot to you. But whatever it is
will fail at first. It will be three or four years, perhaps
more, before you realize the success of it."

Her prediction, delivered in a voice hollow with dread,
made me laugh. I gave the old woman a few small coins
and continued back to the hotel with Von Stroheim.

Macao was completed in the spring of 1939, but was not
released until the fall. Following *Macao*, Von Stroheim
went to work on his last French film before World War II,
Paris-New York, a shipboard drama made entirely on board
the liner *Normandie* during its final Atlantic crossing to
New York before the war began. The famous and ill-fated
luxury steamship returned from New York the latter part
of August.

A few days later, on September 1, 1939, Germany
declared war on Poland and Adolf Hitler's armies began
to march. From London, England's Prime Minister Neville
Chamberlain pronounced in a colorless voice: "We are now
in a state of war with Germany." France rushed into action.

Von Stroheim, high on the Nazi roll of enemies of the
Third Reich, sought refuge in the United States after the
French Army rejected his bid for service. He was followed
by a goodly number of French film notables.

Why Von was scheduled for liquidation by the Germans,
I am not sure. I only know that his famous portrayals of
Prussian officers wounded German vanity deeply. I guess
it was enough that his performance as von Rauffenstein,

the German commandant, in *La Grande Illusion*, antago-
nized Hitler. The German leader, with his aides Himmler,
Goering and Goebbels, saw the film at a special showing
in Berlin. The French government awarded Von the
coveted Legion of Honor in recognition of his magnificent
portrayal. But, speaking for Hitler and the others, Josef
Goebbels denounced Von in a propaganda radio broad-
cast, declaring, "Stroheim's impersonation of a German
officer is a caricature! No German officer is like that!"

Macao, when it was released and shown, received very
good critical notice. Neither Von's part nor mine was
earth-shaking, but both roles gave us an opportunity to
display our depth of artistry. Public acceptance left no
doubt the picture would pay for itself and earn a profit.
Demofilm was very pleased.

But then, suddenly—for the start of a war comes suddenly, when talk abruptly ends and battle begins—German
troops overran France and she surrendered. Paris was
invaded and occupied on June 14, 1940.

That day I watched the victorious Germans march arro-
gantly down the Champs Élysées led by a vanguard of
roaring motorcycles and a line of open automobiles filled
with generals and other high-ranking staff officers. As the
goose-stepping columns of soldiers swept along the boulevard, the tricolor of France waving from the masts of the
buildings lining the thoroughfare was ripped down, and
replaced by the banner of Nazism. The wide sidewalks
were all but deserted. Paris had been declared an open
city when the Germans broke the last of French resistance
in the Marne, and had been evacuated. More dogs than
men wandered its streets. And of the population which
remained, most were old persons to whom fleeing seemed
of little importance.

The Germans did not bother me, for Japan was Hitler's

ally, by sympathy, if not in declared fact. For her warlords, the leaders of the military party, had risen to power, and the inevitable had been plotted. It was only a matter of time until the aggression of the East would begin and mirror that of the West already embarked upon by Hitler and his Nazi Germany.

The Japanese Embassy in Paris issued a call for all nationals, such as myself, to return to Japan. I chose to remain in Paris. I have never been particularly interested in politics. Acting has been my life. But public figures such as actors are touched noticeably by politics and the governmental machinations of their homelands whether or not they wish to be. Public appreciation and affection for them as artists give them a leadership on which politicians desire to trade. I am sure the Japanese government which precipitated the war between Japan and the United States would have demanded my services as an influence. It would have, that is, if I had been in sympathy with the aims of the military party in Japan. I was not. I was strongly opposed to the rule of the warlords. And, although I did not publicly declare myself one way or another, the military party knew my views.

Because of my opposition, I could not return to Japan. To do so would have meant death. No price was put on my head. My name was not put upon a list as Von Stroheim's was by Hitler. But I knew death awaited my return to Japan. My sense of destiny told me to stay in France. So I stayed, even though it was to mean long separation from my wife, son and daughter, and from the daughter who was born after I left Japan and went to Paris to make *Yoshiwara*. I did not see her, not even in a photograph, until she was almost eleven years old.

My wife and I were in communication by letter and cable until the bombing of Pearl Harbor and the start of the war in the Pacific. Then all direct communication was stopped. For months neither of us knew how the other was, or what was happening. All I learned of the war between Japan and the United States was what I read in the Paris newspapers. Carefully tutored by the Germans, the papers printed little truth and much propaganda. The reports I read told me of great Japanese and German victories.

The news did not make me happy. I did not believe what I read. I felt deep within me that it was Japan's destiny to lose her war with the United States. She would be brought to her knees, I was sure. To me, all signs indicated this fate from the beginning of her bid for total rule of the Far East. I knew that her people, my people, did not wish to aggress. Only the military party desired it. It took over Japan just as the Nazi party rose to dominate Germany.

The fall of France and the occupation of Paris brought French motion picture production to a standstill. Distribution and showing continued, however. But *Macao* ceased to be a source of film entertainment on French movie screens.

Shortly after the German high command took control of Paris, I, along with others from Demofilm concerned with the picture, was summoned to German headquarters and informed that *Macao* was not to be shown.

"It is not permitted," the smoothly tailored officer in charge informed us. "Individuals, one in particular, unsympathetic to the cause of our Führer—enemies of Germany, appear in this film," he said in perfect French as we stood uneasy before him. "Hitler is not interested in seeing the German officer lampooned."

"There is no chance then?" I asked.

The officer glanced at me sharply. "You are a neutral, are you not, Mr. Hayakawa?"

"Yes."

"It is best you remain so. That is all. You may go." He rang for his orderly. The door behind us was opened, and we filed out.

I don't know who made the decision, but it was decided to salvage *Macao* in the only manner possible—by replacing all of Von Stroheim's scenes, and there were many, with retakes with another actor.

This was done at considerable cost some two years later, when those who played scenes with Von—Mireille Balin and myself in particular—were recalled by Demofilm. All of Von's scenes were remade with Pierre Renoir playing the role of Werner Krall. Only after this was done did the Nazis allow *Macao* to be shown during the Occupation. Following the Liberation, however, all of Von's scenes were replaced by the French distributors.

The deletion of Von's scenes from his French pictures was not limited to *Macao*. The Germans also cut him out of another of his films, *Derrière la Façade*. The rest of the twenty-four French films he made prior to the German Occupation of France were either burned, banned or buried. *Menaces,* for instance, the picture he made just before *Macao,* was buried by its producers until after the Liberation when it was dug up and released with great success.

The misfortune, delay and expense experienced by Demofilm and me in the matter of *Macao* bore out the prediction the old woman in Nice had made for me. It was not until 1942 that the Nazi-approved version of the picture was circulated; and then with little success, considering the situation. And not until 1947 that the film reached its most lucrative markets, England and the United States. By that time, Von was back in Paris and busy once again making films.

After remaking the necessary scenes for *Macao*, I resumed the passive state in which I spent the war years. I spent a great deal of my time in painting and writing. And wondering about my family, for now Japan was at war with the United States.

To me, personally, the bombing of Pearl Harbor was a crushing humiliation. It made my heart sick. When I read about it in the Paris newspapers, I wanted to cry out, "This is not my Japan! It is the warrior fools who have her throat in their iron fists!"

The attack on Hawaii and the war which followed tore me between two great affections—for Japan and for the United States. I am a Japanese, a son of Nippon. The roots of my family reach deep into her history, as I have said. My love of my native land goes beyond whatever political thought may temporarily rule her. I could not repudiate her, though evil ruled. But, too, my feeling for the United States was great. I have never turned my back on my Japanese heritage, but all that is Western in me I have gained from my life and success in the United States. That my two countries had entered into war was a bitter blow.

What turn of destiny was this, I wondered; to be caught in the middle of a clash of ideologies alien to the path of my life. I had no choice but to endure, to steel myself— my mind—against the disheartening and depressing imprisonment of enforced exile. I meditated to free myself of the sense of being in the here and now of the war with its privation and indescribable horror.

My being a Japanese national in France, with a long record of association and sympathy with the United States, put me in a unique but hardly enviable position when the Germans invaded Paris. I was quite naturally suspected by both sides. The Germans were allied with Japan. But, of course, although dominated in all but spirit by the Germans, the French were allied with England and the United States. Before and after the start of the war between Japan and the United States, I was some sort of an enemy to all. I had to rely, and could only rely, on my neutrality as a citizen of the world, so to speak, to protect me. I thought the French would take violent action against me, if possible; but they did nothing more than give me dubious and cautious looks when I appeared on the streets of Paris and in its public places.

When the Germans came, the British and American nationals in Paris left. But most of the Japanese remained, I among them. Some did heed the edict of the Embassy and made their ways to Lisbon, where a ship waited to take them to Japan. Those who remained were employed at the Embassy, married to French women or possessed business interests well worth protecting. I think, however, that I was the only one whose exile from Japan was in the interest of preserving my life.

Among the Japanese who stayed in Paris were many who hastened to co-operate with the Germans, once they had taken possession of the city. Later, when the Allies liberated the French capital, these people fled. Many of them went to Berlin. When the Allies retook Paris there were only forty Japanese nationals in residence.

Those of us who remained in Paris throughout the German occupation, the neutral and vanquished alike, lived in an atmosphere of indefinable terror. The very air was charged with evil. To relax was unknown. The nightly scream of Gestapo sirens through the dark streets, the thunder of Nazi boots in the hallways and on stairs was unnerving. There was no place to hide but within oneself.

I passed the years until the Germans were driven out, a man on a tightrope. I did nothing to identify myself with Germany's cause and Hitler's mad desires. And I could do little to identify myself with French resistance. Therefore, suspended, I retreated into the world of Zen thought and set myself to move **with the flow of** life as best I could, passively on the middle road, within the morality and humanity of my nature. Only within myself, in Zen, was I able to find the strength to endure. In meditation I sought to put myself outside the pale of war.

"Nothing appears to bother you—nothing," a friend remarked to me one day. "It is as if you live in an oasis in the desert war makes of life."

"I do," I said. "I must!"

"But how? How can you shut yourself off?"

"How, indeed?" I said, and fell to reflecting, contemplating the time when the war would end and a climate in which I could move freely would return.

A sensation of dread I cannot accurately express sweeps over me when I pause to think upon what my life during the war might have been had I not walked in Zen. A man's faith is his rock; and, although Zen is not a faith in the sense of the word which relates the Christian soul with the Christian God, Zen similarly sustains. For Zen frees oneself from oneself, time and circumstance.

On June 10, 1944, I celebrated my fifty-fourth birthday. I naturally thought of home and of my wife and family, from whom I had not heard in nearly three years.

But I did not feel apart from Tsuru and the children. My mind, every fiber of my being, was tuned to them through Zen. Our affinity was preserved, though thousands of miles separated us. I felt their presence vividly. It was as if we were linked by an invisible cord through which every pulse of relationship was transmitted and told me of them. I knew they were well and safe. I would have known if anything happened to them.

Zen keys the mind to the reception of such events as death. I had sensed the death of my mother, for instance, when both my wife and I were ill and in bed with influenza in Hollywood in 1920. I lay in a fever looking at my mother's photograph. And as I gazed upon her likeness the feeling that my mother was no longer in the realm of human existence swept over me. I involuntarily shook. "She is gone," I said to Tsuru. "My mother is dead. I shall not see her again." A letter from my elder brother arrived a few days later and confirmed what I already knew.

By mid-1944, the course of the war changed. For almost a year the Allied armed forces of the United States, Great Britain and those of the Free French under General de Gaulle, had been on the offensive. The Germans and Italians had been turned back in North Africa. Rommel, the Desert Fox, had been taxed to the breaking point and defeated. The Allies had landed in Italy and tediously advanced up through that tortured country driving the enemy back while other forces struck at the French channel coast, landed at Normandy and began the steady, costly push inland. Suddenly Hitler got a glimpse of the future. His star began to descend.

The fighting in Normandy threw Paris into a furor. The smug and superior confidence of the Germans began to fade. Throughout the city ran an undercurrent of anticipation. One could smell liberation in the hot summer air.

On August 25, 1944, a combined force of American and French soldiers entered the city. Not long after, I once again stood to watch a victorious army march along the Champs Élysées. I stood on the same spot, near my apartment, from which I had silently, unemotionally viewed the revolting strut and swagger of the Germans four years before. Now, happily, I saw long lines of Americans and French and English. And on the sidewalks, wild with joy, radiant and jubilant, cheering French. Now the flags being torn from their moorings were those of the Nazis. In place of them the French tricolor was proudly restored.

After the parade broke up, the boulevard was jammed

with a blur of constantly moving uniforms and civilian dress. Flowers were everywhere. And where there were flowers there were girls, delirious with joy, hugging and kissing the soldiers. I roared welcome along with the rest of Paris and, later, when the tumult died down somewhat, approached a soldier here and there, introduced myself and invited him to enjoy the comfort of my apartment.

I recall that one young man looked at me in amazement when I stopped him and spoke in English. "Hell, man, you're not French. Who are you?" he said.

When I told him my name he grinned and slapped his head. "Hey, Jerry!" he bellowed to a friend. "Who is Sessue Hayakawa?"

Embarrassed, I explained who I was.

"This guy's a movie actor," the young soldier informed his companion. "Says we can use his place to take a bath."

I smiled, nodding. "My apartment is yours."

"Well, how about that. Mr. Hayakawa, sir, lead on."

"A little food will be in order, too," I remarked as I led him and his friend Jerry to my apartment. En route, two or three others joined us. We moved along the street like a happy cloud. Laughter and tears were everywhere we looked. Every man in uniform, American and Free French, was a hero. How the French of Paris loved them! My pride welled as I watched their reception. Seeing the American troops brought back many happy memories.

In my apartment, while I supervised the preparation of something to eat, I could hear my guests laughing and joking as they took turns splashing in the bathtub. They swore good-naturedly and snapped each other with the bath towels.

Unlike the haughty Germans, the men who marched shoulder to shoulder along the Champs Élysées, filling it from curb to curb, were playful and boisterous in spirit, open-faced, warm and friendly. They smiled and laughed.

They conjured gaiety and an abandon of happiness where, in 1940, the ominous, obscene tread of the heavy boots of Hitler's warriors, their cold gaze and mechanical movement, had struck terror and stretched hope thin.

But now the tide had turned. The flags of freedom were once again blowing in the cool wind sweeping along the wide boulevards of Paris and across her spacious intersections—Place de l'Opéra, where the famous Café de la Paix again sprang to life in the shadow of the famed Opera House; Place de la Concorde, at the foot of the Champs Élysées and the head of the Tuileries where the Louvre is; Place Saint-Germain des Près, across the Seine, on the fabled Left Bank, where the cafés of the 1920's, made famous by many Americans of yesteryear residence in Paris, the Flore, the Deux Magots, Lipp—all rang with celebration.

After the Germans were driven out of Paris, I saw something that became a common occurrence as the French hunted and arrested collaborators. As more and more Allied troops entered Paris, parades took place regularly. I often watched. One day, when I was standing in front of my hotel watching some troops march by, I saw a nude woman walking toward me. She was surrounded by a mob of jeering French housewives and young boys and girls. At first I thought the nude figure was some sort of statue, or someone wearing very snug flesh-colored circus tights. Every contour of her body was revealed.

But as the yelling mob and the woman neared, I saw that she was absolutely naked except for shoes—high heels in which she stumbled along the rough cobblestones of the street. She was quite beautiful, I thought, although her head had been shaved bald. And her figure was magnificent.

"The pig preferred to sleep with a German officer," the man next to me said when I asked him what was going on.

The woman passed by, the mob driving her down the street with howls of insult.

This humiliating retribution I saw many times. Each was a strange scene indeed. But then, what is stranger than war and its aftermath?

In November, 1944, Winston Churchill announced in London: "All Hitler's satellites have turned against him. The slaves driven so far against their interests, against their honor, against—in many cases—their inclinations, have had the chance to turn against the slave-driver and may now wreak a vengeance." With these words, it became evident that Germany was losing the war, and the conflict in Europe would soon come to an end.

The fighting in Europe finally came to an end in May, 1945. But war still raged, horrible and bitter, in the Pacific. And now, as the Allies celebrated the defeat of Nazi Germany, I wondered what the attitude of the French and Americans would be toward me.

Curiously enough, the American soldiers who first approached me after Paris was retaken were friendly. They treated me as one of their own—Sessue Hayakawa, the famous American motion picture star. I had the pleasure of entertaining them at dinner and allowing them the use of my bathtub, which, next to a bottle of good cognac, was the greatest luxury in Paris. One thing the Americans and Japanese have in common is the love of a good hot bath.

The GI's who accepted my hospitality were very cordial. Not once did they talk pointedly about the fighting in the Pacific or treat me as though I were one of the enemy.

But I thought about the fighting there a great deal. I knew it was only a matter of time until it, too, would end. But, like millions of others who reasoned this way, I knew nothing of how it would end.

Then, on August 6, 1945, the first atomic bomb was

dropped on Hiroshima, and more than 78,000 persons died in the blinding hot flash it made. The second, killing more than 73,000 thousand, was dropped three days later, on Nagasaki, as destiny would have it, the city where Christianity first took hold in Japan. On August 14 Japan surrendered.

Was it necessary? I asked the question the day I read of the Hiroshima bombing in Paris. I still ask it. I think the bombing of Hiroshima was inhuman, just as I think that of Pearl Harbor was inhuman. There was a frantic soullessness behind both acts. I still cannot understand why the United States dropped the bomb into the city. The power of it could just as well have been demonstrated by exploding it in the nearby mountains or, better, in the bay. I think a display of the power of the atomic bomb would have yielded the same result of surrender. The obliteration of thousands of innocent women and children and men is something I cannot conceive of producing good, even though the cause of their deaths ended the war.

After the surrender of Japan and the American occupation there began, I received word of my wife and family for the first time in more than five years. American friends, serving in the forces of occupation, called on them and wrote word of the safety and well-being of my family to other friends in the United States. They, in turn, relayed the good news to others in Paris who told me. We still could not communicate directly. Not until some years later was I permitted to send word. And then it was restricted to a message on a postcard written either in English or French. Japanese was not permitted.

In the fall of 1945, as France struggled to return to normalcy, I resumed my activities as an actor. My French had vastly improved during the Occupation, and when the film studios opened, I proceeded to make some more pictures. I wanted to return to Japan and to my family, but the authorities would not permit this. I had no difficulty traveling about Europe, however. In 1947, I went to Venice and was a judge at the International Film Festival there. The following year, to my surprise, Hollywood suddenly became interested in me. A silence of nearly sixteen years was broken when I received a cable from Humphrey Bogart, who wanted me for a picture. About to make *Tokyo Joe*, for Columbia Pictures, he made a specific request of the studio that I be signed to appear in it with him.

"From what I remember of him, he's perfect for the part," he told Robert Lord, the producer. "I want him to do it with me, so get him!"

Robert Lord took a dubious view of my qualifications, for he cabled the Paris offices of Columbia: "Is Hayakawa too old and feeble to stage a good fight with Bogart?"

The Columbia Pictures representative in Paris located and called on me bearing this message.

"Try hitting me on the chin," I told him, smiling. I let my arms hang at my sides. The man balked at the idea, but when I assured him nothing would happen he rushed at me and swung. I blocked his arm, snapped it around and was about to flip him down when he yelled for me to stop. I freed him and laughed. He informed Lord there was little doubt about my giving Bogart a good fight. After a couple of cables, I was signed to do *Tokyo Joe*.

Now the problem was for me to return to the United States. To be allowed to return, that is. I took my passport and went to the American Embassy.

"I think you know as well as I, Mr. Hayakawa, that this is next to worthless," the official at the embassy said when I requested a visa and he thumbed through my passport. "Technically, my country and yours are still at war. The

fighting has ended, as you know, but no peace treaty has
been signed."

"What can I do?" I asked.

"Let me look into the matter. After all, you have had
quite a career in the United States. I'm sure something
can be done."

He said he would get in touch with me. He did so a few
weeks later, and when I again conferred with him in his
office, he said:

"You check out all right according to the Civilian Investi-
gation Department. You'll probably be surprised to learn
we have a file on your activities all during the Occupation.
Do you recall the time a friend of yours became ill on stage
and you tried to get an ambulance?"

"You know about that?" I said, somewhat dumbfounded.

"We know you refused to ask the Germans for help."

This incident had taken place some years before. A
Japanese actor friend of mine was taken sick during a
performance I attended. When I sought to get an ambulance for him, it was suggested, since Japan was allied with
Germany, that I ask the Germans for aid. "I don't want to
ask the Germans," I had replied hotly. Since getting a
French ambulance was virtually impossible, I ended by
using my influence to get the Japanese Embassy to send a
car. Even then the situation was awkward. Nevertheless,
what I did was in my favor when the American State
Department investigated.

I was cleared for re-entry into the United States by all
concerned. Particularly the U. S. Army and the State
Department. And a special visa was issued to me. Therefore, on December 31, 1948, I found myself airborne for
New York. There friends waited to celebrate my return
and the advent of the new year with a party.

10 The Cup of Humanity

THE FLIGHT ACROSS THE ATLANTIC WAS UNEVENTFUL, BUT snow and severe headwinds kept the plane from arriving at New York on time. After a short stop for fuel at Gander, Newfoundland, we flew on to Boston where, through swirling snow, I got my first glimpse of the United States in sixteen years. After we landed, the storm kept us grounded for most of the hours I had expected to spend celebrating the arrival of the New Year and my return with my friends in New York. It was nearly dawn when we finally got back into the air. I marked the coming of 1949 while sitting in the Boston airport lounge.

The plane reached New York about 5:00 A.M. The party planned for my arrival had gone on without me. My friends were all home in bed. I made my way into Manhattan alone, on the airport bus, and checked into the Sherry-Netherland Hotel, at Fifty-ninth Street and Fifth Avenue, where Columbia Pictures had reserved a suite.

The war in the Pacific had been over for more than three years, but I could not help feeling that the reaction of the American public to me as a Japanese would be anything but cold. I did not expect any mass demonstration against me, but I did fear that some isolated instance of hostility would occur.

The lobby of the hotel was still peopled with New Year's celebrants when I arrived from the airport. Parties were ending. Guests and hosts were going to breakfast. Most were in evening dress. Among them, I stood out boldly. I was dressed for travel, in a comfortable sportcoat and a pair of slacks.

However, I attracted little attention when I signed the hotel register and the desk clerk called my name as he ordered the bellman to take my luggage to the elevator. No one gave me more than a passing glance. It was a relief not to be singled out.

I was tired, but too excited to sleep. After unpacking and cleaning myself up a bit, I was eager to see New York and to call old friends.

I wanted very much to see Broadway, and to walk in Times Square and around the theatre district. Fifth Avenue was bare of traffic. The doorman shrugged when I asked for a taxi. None was in sight. It was snowing, and a bitter winter wind was blowing.

But I wouldn't be put off. I began walking down Fifth Avenue, and eventually turned west and made my way to Times Square. The lights there were still bright. The sidewalks were crowded. The restaurants were full.

The morning papers carried my picture and announced my return to the United States with headlines such as: "Sessue Hayakawa Back in U.S. Will Play in Film with Bogart." I wasn't in Times Square very long before I was recognized and approached.

"Aren't you Sessue Hayakawa, the actor?" one fellow

who saw me asked. I nodded and smiled, and was surprised and delighted to find total strangers warmly welcoming me back. Older people who remembered me from my silent pictures stopped to say hello and wish me a Happy New Year.

I had worried for nothing. Everywhere I went, when I was recognized, I was shown kindness. Perhaps it was the holiday spirit. But whether or not it was, everyone was friendly. I enjoyed my walk and returned to the hotel and went to bed.

Too excited to sleep much, I awoke around noon and telephoned my lawyer. He joined me in my suite and we talked the afternoon away. I was pleased to learn from him that I wouldn't have to worry about money. He had collected and banked the rent for my house in Great Neck all the years I was caught in France. After more than a decade the account was quite large.

That evening, he and I went to Chinatown, where I enjoyed the best dinner I had eaten in years. After that, we talked some more. Two days later, on January 3, I left for Hollywood by plane.

When I returned to Hollywood after an absence of sixteen years, the film critics, publicity agents and newspaper columnists promptly hailed my return as one from retirement and oblivion. It was announced that I was making a comeback.

This has happened a number of times. I have never really understood why. Considering that I made seventeen motion pictures in France, before and after the war, and appeared in four major stage productions in Paris, the "triumphant return of a silent screen idol," as one writer commented, was no return or comeback. I was merely continuing my professional activities.

But Hollywood buries its actors and actresses when they

leave to work elsewhere. At least it used to consider them out of the limelight. In Hollywood, you're only as good as your last picture.

Presently, however, motion pictures, television and the stage are so interrelated and dependent upon one another that, fortunately, one no longer dies professionally when the Hollywood colony is put behind for activity elsewhere.

But then, in 1949, I was heralded as staging a comeback and given the indulgent "welcome back" treatment. Representatives of Columbia Pictures met me at International Airport in Burbank and drove me on a tour before taking me to the studio. I will admit I didn't recognize Hollywood at all. The hills where I had ridden my horse in the silent days were dotted with housing; the streets and freeways— all built since I had been there last—were crowded with cars. Everything had changed but the oil wells. The towers still stuck up in strange places—some right inside the studios.

Finally I was taken to the studio and introduced to Humphrey Bogart, whom I had never met. He was most kind. "I have admired you for years," he said. "It's going to be good working with you."

Humphrey Bogart and I got along very well together right from the start. It was a great compliment to me that, although there were any number of Japanese and Chinese actors in Hollywood, any one of whom might have been offered the role I was asked to play, he insisted on having me.

We completed filming *Tokyo Joe* in about eight weeks. Once more, I was the villain—an *intransigeant* postwar Japanese, who refused to accept defeat. As usual, I died a violent death.

I was supposed to return to Paris to make a film, but after *Tokyo Joe* was finished my stock in Hollywood was high. I was asked to join Claudette Colbert in *Three Came Home*, a picture based on the real life adventures of an American wife and her children in a Borneo prisoner-of-war camp during the Japanese occupation. Jean Negulesco directed it for Twentieth Century-Fox.

It was while I was making this picture that I experienced a mental and physical reaction unlike any ever experienced before. It recalled the intense pain that followed my attempt at hara-kiri, and revealed to me a sensation of empathy I had not known I possessed.

When I was in Paris in the early 1920's, I frequently attended the ballet and saw Anna Pavlova dance *The Swan* many times.

The first performance I saw of this ballet overwhelmed me completely. Afterwards I went backstage to congratulate her, and I asked her: "When you sink to the stage and slowly cease to flutter as the swan, you seem to actually die. It's so real. How do you do it?"

She smiled sadly at my question. "My heart actually stops at that moment. When I am conscious of my acting—my dancing—I cannot die. But when I completely become the dying bird my heart stops. Death is expressed completely at that moment—for a moment."

What Pavlova's explanation meant to me was that only when such a state of selflessness and unconscious action is attained, when an actor becomes the character being played, is great art produced.

In *Three Came Home*, I portrayed a Japanese army colonel in command of a prisoner-of-war camp in Borneo. In one scene I receive word from Japan that my three children have been killed. Outside my quarters at the prison camp three of the prisoners' children are playing. When I look from the letter that has brought me the tragic news, I see them and in my mind see my own children. The scene outside my quarters melts me completely. I take the three children and see that they are fed and try to make them happy.

When I played this scene something deep within me snapped. Tears rolled down my cheeks as I watched the playing children and thought in reaction to the news in the letter from Japan. Suddenly I felt as if a great hand had grasped my intestines and was twisting them. In that moment, before the camera, I was not Hayakawa at all. I was that wretched Japanese colonel crying at his loss, trying pitifully to solace himself in doing a kindness. After thirty-five years a depth unknown to me before was plumbed. I suddenly knew what Pavlova meant when she said that her heart stopped. It was a great discovery for me, but in a way I feel it came too late.

Being back in Hollywood afforded me the chance of renewing a number of old acquaintances and friendships, among them one I enjoyed making many years before in the south of France. There, one day on the beach at Nice, I met a charming young girl. She was a timid creature— shy, I think, because of her feeling of inferiority to the wealthy young people she found herself among. Her family was not rich or particularly prominent in society. I was her sympathetic friend of two summers, before I returned to New York late in 1925. Thereafter, we lost contact until I went to Hollywood to make *Tokyo Joe* and *Three Came Home*. Shortly after the latter was finished, I was delighted to receive a telephone call from her. She was now married to an American and was living in San Francisco. And would I, she asked, join her and her husband for a holiday in Las Vegas?

I accepted, and the three of us drove to Las Vegas, where she and her husband had rented a bungalow for the summer.

I had a very good time with them—at first. We went

swimming, lounged and talked during the day; and at night visited the nightclubs and the gambling casinos.

I no sooner got into the casinos than my gambler's fever came to the fore. I got a pair of dice in my hand and the nights were claimed.

I gambled three or four nights in a row, winning and losing. I was genial during the day, but something happened at night. I lost control and began to shoot money away as if it were going out of style.

One evening, after I had been at the dice table for hours, but had finally torn myself free, I arrived at the bungalow to find my friend waiting for me. She was crying, and when I asked her if she had perhaps quarreled with her husband, she shook her head.

"Then why are you crying?" I asked.

She sat there looking at me for a long time. "Can I tell you the truth?" she said finally.

"Yes, tell me. Is it something I have done? You are usually so cheerful. This crying I don't understand. Why?"

She said, "Sessue, my tears are not from sadness or a fight with my husband, but from heartache."

"Are you ill?"

"No." She paused and lighted a cigarette. "I knew you years ago in France. You were very kind to me in Nice. We had good times together. And when I read you were back in the United States, in Hollywood, my first impulse was to call you and ask you to join us here. I've always admired and respected you. You are one of the finest men I know. But since you came here to Las Vegas . . . I just don't know. I've watched your face when you've stood at the tables shooting crap, and you've become a completely changed man—hard and cruel. You look like a devil! I can't stand to see you look like that. You're not the man I knew when I was little. I'm sorry, but that's why I'm crying. I know it seems silly, but . . ."

"I didn't think it meant that much," I said. "I should be sorry. I gamble for amusement. I always have. But if you feel the way that you do . . . well, I'll quit gambling."

And I did quit. I have not gambled since that incident in Las Vegas.

When I returned to Hollywood to act with Humphrey Bogart, I had left things in Paris somewhat at loose ends. I expected to return there to star in a film titled *Red God*. But while I was working on *Three Came Home*, the head of a Japanese film company contacted me and insisted I go back to Japan and make a film there. I accepted his offer and cabled Paris not to expect me.

The short time I spent in Hollywood was half work and half holiday. I received numerous invitations to parties, and recalling the fun we had in the old silent days, I got around as much as possible.

I remember one party in particular. I had passed most of the evening on the sidelines. But by the time coffee was served I had begun to talk about Zen and acting to a group of young actresses who were doing their best to be noticed.

I was talking casually, but the more I talked, the more pointed the discussion became.

In the group I found around me was a young girl of about twenty. She was a very pretty girl. But as she sat listening, her eyes filled with tears. It was obvious something was troubling her, for when the party ended she told me: "I would very much like to hear you more. May I come and see you?"

"If you wish, come by my hotel in a day or two."

A few days later she came to call accompanied by her mother.

"You told us the other night that as long as we have a conscious mind we cannot be true artists."

I nodded.

"If so, what becomes of the conscious mind," she went on, "when we are concerned with too many worries? You advised us to reduce our minds to nothingness. Does it mean that to have a genuine, carefree mind is to have a mind like that of a little child?"

"You cried the other night at the party. Are you worried?" I asked her.

"Yes. Several days ago I was recommended to Paramount as a co-star for Bing Crosby, but after the producer talked with him, they decided I looked too gloomy for the role. They said I was too serious and that I couldn't smile. I don't know how they expect me to be happy when I have so many personal problems."

"You must remember that your personal problems are not their concern."

"Well, I just don't feel like being happy. I want to be, but I don't feel like it."

While she spoke I looked at her mother. She sat in a corner frowning, and I imagined most of the actress' problems had to do with her. The mother looked to me like a person given to continual criticism and carping, who was discouraging her daughter. For the next hour I talked about the tolerance that is necessary if a person is to develop naturally. Practically everything I said hit home. By the time I finished, both mother and daughter were crying.

"I don't ask you to stop crying," I said. "Cry as much as you like. We will talk some more when you're finished."

Finally the mother admitted she had been wrong about her daughter. "I've wanted her to be a serious person," she said, "and I guess I've been too severe."

"Because of the strict way you've raised me I lost a good chance at a good job," the daughter put in.

I recognized this was an old argument, so I turned the conversation away from the concrete aspects of life. "If, some morning when I awake, I choose to wear a bright tie," I said, "that particular morning I am happy and in a joyous mood. However, if I select another tie, one in dark subdued colors, I am most likely disturbed and melancholy. People seem to dress according to the way they feel. Especially women. In your case, you're wearing a black dress and a hat with a veil. You look as if you are on the way home from a funeral. Why don't you wear a gay costume and a big hat with a ribbon? Look happy and enjoy yourself. No wonder you didn't get the part. If you went to see Bing Crosby looking as you do today, he probably thought. . . . Who knows what he thought?

"Go see him again," I said, "and wait to see him if you have to sit all day. And dress as if you are happy."

A day or two passed. The girl came back to see me. She was wearing a colorful print dress and a big straw sailor hat with a red ribbon. She was cheerful and gay, an entirely different person.

"Anything develop?" I asked.

She took a piece of official-looking paper out of her pocket and waved it at me. "This! Read this!" It was a contract. "I went to see Mr. Crosby and the producer wearing this costume, and knocked them for a loop," she cried excitedly. "They found it hard to believe I was the same person."

I guess the story of the plain girl who suddenly is transformed into a beauty when she removes her glasses and lets down her hair is one of the oldest Hollywood clichés. But things of this sort do happen. It was quite obvious to me that my little friend, prodded by her mother, was trying to be something she was not. When she stopped playing a role that didn't suit her and was what her youth and beauty indicated she should be, she got the job she wanted.

The story of what happened when the girl followed my advice circulated around Hollywood and prompted one of the studio public relations men to arrange for me to speak to various groups of women in Los Angeles on the subject of the unity of spiritual and physical aspects of life.

At one meeting I was asked: "When you are at a cocktail party, Mr. Hayakawa, don't you usually notice and talk with just the pretty women present? Or do you find yourself charmed by the plain-looking woman. Do they attract you as well?"

The following was my reply:

The last time I was in Paris—before the war, that is—I frequently played golf at the links in Saint-Cloud. In the course of making a round one afternoon I noticed a dowdy, quite unattractive Japanese woman on the course. She was taking lessons from the club professional, I later learned; and I asked him to introduce me to her. He did so, referring to her as "Countess Asa."

I could not fathom what it was at the time, but something about the woman fascinated me. I asked her to try the course with me; and after we played a few holes, I invited her to join me at tea.

Tea among the Japanese is a delicate and tradition-governed ritual. The taking of it according to prescribed formalities is part of the Japanese art of life. Tea in the world of the East is, simply, the cup of humanity which bridges distances not otherwise spanned.

The Countess Asa poured tea for me in the Japanese manner, with an elegance and grace which belied her plain appearance. She displayed a mastery of conversation. I was deeply impressed by the cast of nobleness with which her face was illuminated. My impression of her was one entirely different from that I had when we first met on the golf course, and I thought what an unusual person she was. I invited her to play a round with me the following day, and took leave of her feeling I had met someone whose outward appearance little indicated true character.

A few days passed, and one evening when I was playing bridge with Viscount Katano and his bride, who were visiting Paris on their wedding trip, he remarked, "Next time, we should play at Asa's, and afterwards have dinner together." Eventually, they took me there, where I was surprised to hear a guest, a general, address the plain woman I knew as Countess Asa as, "Your Royal Highness." When I commented on this it was explained that she was not the Countess Asa, but Princess Asaka, third daughter of the Emperor Meiji. She preferred to be called Countess rather than have to go through the countless tedious formalities incumbent on her rank. She was a plain woman indeed, but her royal blood and aristocratic up-bringing shone in her regal manner. She was very well liked, and when I came to know her better I found her a warm, outgoing person who effortlessly made one feel at ease. Whatever the Princess Asaka lacked in the way of physical attractiveness was of small importance in comparison with the charm of her personality.

One's looks and figure make an important first impression. But when that is over and done, how one behaves becomes infinitely more important. What you are is a matter of the mind. If you have a beautiful soul and a good personality, all that you possess inwardly will reveal itself unconsciously. I find beauty in human beings only when such inward beauty of spirit is revealed in outward appearance and conduct.

While I related this story I observed the women who listened—Western women, Occidentals who, I think, have considerable advantage over Oriental women in the matter of being beautiful.

I have traveled a great deal in the course of my career, and have observed all sorts of women. Beauty is associated with Japanese women, but they are at a disadvantage. All

Oriental women are. Orientals, in general, have black hair; and people with black hair suffer by comparison with those who have **blond** or red hair. Since I paint I see vivid contrast in colors. Japanese are physically restricted to two colors, black hair and eyes and yellow skin.

But in France and the United States, or anywhere in Europe, women are surrounded by color. The feeling received from color is very important. Occidental women have a great weapon for attractiveness in color and the opportunity to vary it in their hair and lips and in what they wear. A Japanese woman does not possess this weapon. They used to wear colorful kimonos, but they have today adopted more conservative and Western modes of dress which lessen their luster. To make up for the loss of color the Japanese woman has one quality. It is her inner beauty, a quality which is indescribable, but evident when experienced. It consists of a gentleness, a silence eloquent with understanding, a wordless obedience. It is a quality no Western woman can imitate.

After completing *Three Came Home,* I left Hollywood for Tokyo by plane. En route across the Pacific, we made short stops at Honolulu and at Wake Island. At Wake I got off the plane to have breakfast and walk along the beach. I saw grim reminders of the war there, among them a Japanese boat half sunk in the wet sand, shell-torn and rusting. It was not a happy sight. Seeing it and remembering and imagining subdued my spirits. I returned to the plane and kept to myself throughout the rest of the flight.

A cheering crowd of five hundred awaited my arrival at Haneda International Airport outside Tokyo, and surged forward against the police lines when my plane touched down and rolled to a stop. The crowd, which included a delegation of noted actors and actresses, the flags waving, a **band playing—was** all a wonderful surprise.

The authorities allowed my family, followed by a horde of newspaper reporters and photographers, to greet me inside the plane. Tsuru cried as I pulled her to me and kissed her. Before the war I might have stood aloof and she would have welcomed me with a bow. But the times had changed. How much they had changed I was about to learn.

Seeing my children astounded me. My son was no longer a boy, but a man. A child of eight when I left Japan for France, he was now twenty. His maturity confused me; and that of my daughters, young ladies now, rather than girls, as well. I hardly recognized my daughters.

The immediate events of my return left my family and me no time to be by ourselves. We were whisked away to a reception at the Grand Hotel in Yokohama, then driven home to Tokyo. Until late that night my house was crowded with visitors. Friends and other well-wishers streamed in and out. It was hours before we were left alone and were able to sit down to the first real Japanese dinner I had had in a decade. Then, finally, I was able to put on a kimono and sit as my father had sat, at the head of the table, surrounded by my family, and sip sake and know that I was at last home. I gloried in being reunited with my family. We celebrated, and began recapturing what the long years of war and separation had necessarily repressed and made dormant.

"The old Japan is fast passing away," I was told when I asked what life was like now that the war was over and foreign occupation had been experienced.

It was evident from the first that I had come home to a new Japan—a fast-paced, Americanized nation. I found the general atmosphere one of informality. I saw this was good in some ways, but depressing and even revolting in others.

My memory was of Japan before the war. Then the

traditions of centuries were still rigidly in force. Wives followed husbands at a discreet distance when walking in public. Affection was reserved for a private time and place. Friends bowed when they met. There was a reserve and a strict formality. Protocol governed just about everything.

But the loss of the war and the occupation changed all that. The great cartels and monopolies of commerce and manufacture were broken up. The great landholdings were dissolved—those of my family among them. The spirit of democracy was introduced and defined as equality. An emancipation from heritage and tradition suddenly took place.

The change is still going on. But I think it has occurred too quickly and violently. The introduction of democracy into Japan under the armed forces occupation commanded by General MacArthur was a good thing, but not in all ways. The freedom he allowed gave rise to bad as well as good. Under its influence I have seen the Japan I loved, the Japan of old, pushed aside and replaced with a movement and tempo of life too fast for organization.

11   A Soundless Sound

THUS FAR, I HAVE WRITTEN ABOUT MY LIFE AND CAREER IN the world of birth and death, the sphere of existence as it is physically known to man, in terms of time—day, month and year. But in truth I do not live by the calendar. Time as man conceives it is a mundane restraint which confines man and makes him its slave. Time governs mercilessly. But only if you let it.

In Zen there is no time. Everything is based upon the infinite and the eternal. The calendar has no place or function. It is recorded that Buddha said: "Life is instantaneous, and living is dying. Just as the chariot-wheel in rolling rolls only at one point of the tire, and in resting rests at one point; in the same way the life of a living being lasts only for the period of one thought. As soon as that thought has ceased, the being is said to have ceased." Therefore, as we think we die or cease to be, and in the same moment

flourish anew. What has time to do with this state?
Nothing.

Time, the very word, is one of many and varied mean-
ings. When I refer to time it is in the sense that time is
continued existence, a matter of duration, the marking of
years and the effect of their passage on persons and things.
Man has made time a necessity, and the divisions of it
according to a mathematical scheme a convenience which
ultimately frustrates and binds. This view of time produces the consciousness of age and its increase. But why
should we be conscious of the calendar? Of what necessity
is it to be conscious of age?

Age is a state of mind. People insist upon holding to
preconceptions of how one should act at a given age.
Making themselves slaves to time, they move automatically
in the world of birth and death slowly and inexorably
through the stages of being that blind custom has ruled
must be—babyhood, childhood, youth, middle and old age—
to a state of decrepitude and the inevitable outcome of such
slavery: Death.

The conceptions of age and the state of being peculiar
to an existence for a certain number of years are the results
of conditioning and the vividness of impression. For example, if you are in grammar school and you see the teacher,
who is thirty, say, you think that to be thirty is to be old.
Then, when you meet a person of fifty or sixty the impression is one of extreme old age. This impression lingers and
unconsciously carries through until you, yourself, have
passed fifty or sixty summers. And you think about your
years and feel you must be old, and your thoughts mold
you physically. You are sixty and you have the idea that
you must act sixty; and since conditioning has impressed
you that sixty is old, you succumb to the concept. Your
shoulders droop and become rounded. Your bones become
feeble. Flesh hangs loose upon them. All this is the result

of a consciousness of relativity. You live sixty years and out of your first impression believe that sixty years is old and you must be old and must assume the characteristics of age.

Not long ago, I·gave an interview in which the reporter described me: "Hayakawa is reportedly seventy years old, jovially admits only forty-five, looks not much older than that. . . ." I think forty-five, I act forty-five, I am forty-five. I grow no older. And I shall not pass away from the being I am now until I am one hundred and forty-five, because, for me, time has come to a stop.

I have followed the way of Zen for more than half a century as time is reckoned in the noninfinite. I have studied and I have practiced, the whole and sole purpose being for me to understand, realize and perfect my own mind; to get beyond the superfluous first layer of my mind to the inner core, the very nature of the mind. That nature is self-awareness, not the function of knowing, but knowing itself.

Dressed in a black kimono, I meditate for at least an hour each day. Sometimes just before retiring or just after awaking from sleep. Through meditation I make my mind a blank. But it is not blankness in the sense of nothingness. It is rather a fullness in that all the poisons which make the ordinary being a slave to time and the world of birth and death are banished. In it, I am emancipated from the encumbrances of ego—the conscious thinking self which makes a distinction between itself and all else.

To live peacefully and happily one must rid oneself of all the unnecessary and destroying emotions. They do destroy, for these emotions of fear, hate and envy work upon us physically through the mind.

When you are ill, your illness affects everyone about you. You communicate the unhappiness you feel to others, so that they as well as you suffer. Truly, mental attitude influences surroundings. If you experience evil emotions, the only result will be evil. Such emotions must be chased from the mind by concentration. Thus is the mind purified.

It is my experience that most of the persons I have known have been so filled with unnecessary emotions like hate, fear and envy that they are unable to live in peace. They cannot detach themselves from the common consciousness of life. They let almost everything that happens to them gnaw at them as a dog gnaws upon a bone. They have to fight—struggle for happiness, and make such a task of life that, in the end, for all they achieve, life seems hollow.

To be free as an individual you must know inner peace. And the only way to know such peace is to know your inner self, the very core of your being beneath the distortions of ego, the false values engendered by blind misconceptions and conditionings influenced by material beliefs.

Buddha said: "I have recognized the deepest truth, which is sublime and peace-giving, but difficult to understand; for most men move in a sphere of worldly interests and find their delight in worldly desires. The worldling will not understand the doctrine, for to him there is happiness in selfhood only, and the bliss that lies in complete surrender to truth is unintelligible to him. He will call resignation what to the enlightened mind is the purest joy. He will see annihilation where the perfected one finds immortality. He will regard as death what the conqueror of self knows to be life everlasting. The truth remains hidden from him who is in the bondage of hate and desire. Nirvana remains incomprehensible to the vulgar whose minds are beclouded with worldly interests."

Shortly after I returned to Japan in 1949, one concept in particular came to occupy my mind. I had never felt that the Japanese, as a people, possessed a truly religious turn of mind. Their attitude in this regard I thought far less pronounced in comparison to religious attitudes of other nationalities, especially the American, with which I am most familiar. Japanese generally go to church only if there is a funeral. If they pray, they pray selfishly for family prosperity and good health. I strongly felt, when I again became acquainted with my people after World War II, that they lacked a sense of morality. They possessed such a sense once. I grew up in light of it. But the war and the rush of new civilization, the introduction of new materialistic ideas and ideals which followed, seemed to me to have erased it.

Feeling as I did, I was compelled to take action to combat the lack. Some ten years before, I had written a play, *The Life of Buddha*. It had been published but never played. I undertook to produce it, my main purpose being to bring and give to people something to think about in life in much the same manner the Passion Plays of Europe do. I wanted to provide my audiences with a spiritual experience and uplift them as I have been uplifted and sustained by my embrace and practice of Zen.

To go the way of Zen and to walk with Buddha is to be without hate, incapable of hating. It is to love selflessly and impartially. It is a blessing.

But a blessing is only half a blessing if kept to oneself. It is natural and obligatory, I think, for one who has felt the hand of Buddha, heard its soundless sound of peace, to wish that others, too, might achieve a similar experience. For no matter how slight the acquaintance one has with Buddha, that person is a better person for having it.

One idea among those in Zen is that fulfillment is not complete, nor can it be complete unless all others approach enlightenment and nirvana as well. I wrote my play and I produced it with the hope that it would open closed minds to truth, eyes to beauty, and make gentle hearts that seemed to me to be barren of love, but full of hatred, jealousy and distrust.

I chose the story of Buddha as the best example of what can strike at the evil in minds and drive out the poisons which cause unhappiness in life. I believed that after seeing his story brought to life upon the stage people without hope and who were suffering by resisting life would realize their faults and would begin anew with love in their hearts.

I financed the production of *The Life of Buddha* with my own money, and depended upon contributions, as well as ticket sales, to make it a success financially. Those in the audiences who were impressed and spiritually moved by the play did donate money. They threw it at the stage, but most of the coins fell short and into the orchestra pit. Thus the musicians got the benefit while the play went into the red and remained there.

The Life of Buddha was an artistic triumph, but a financial failure. We toured extensively, but lost money everywhere we played.

However, the idea of making a profit was a secondary consideration. I was much more interested in raising the moral standard of the Japanese. I was happy to have even two or three persons out of the hundreds who saw the play go away set free from their burdens of worry and anxiety.

As a production, *The Life of Buddha*, though it sought to impart an insight into the problems of those who saw it, was not without problems of its own. I regret to say that my leading lady was not so concerned with the message we attempted to bring as I was.

The last scene of the play was a beautiful and moving one of Buddha achieving his deliverance from worldly bonds and ascending to oneness in eternity. At that moment an angel appeared and sang as Buddha was bathed in an aura of brilliant white backlighting.

One evening, as I sat onstage in the role of Buddha and actress Toshiko Sekiya made her appearance as the angel and began to sing, a strange clicking noise echoed in the silence which marked the scene. My face was composed in the benign expression of Buddha, but I opened my eyes a hair and slowly gazed around in an attempt to discover the source of the spell-breaking noise. I was chagrined to see the angel wearing high heels! Not only that, but in her course of crossing the stage she tripped on the cord leading to the lights providing the radiance behind me. The stage was abruptly plunged into total darkness and the entire closing effect of the play ruined. The curtain came down. I did not move, but sat and waited for Miss Sekiya to come and apologize. Time passed. It became evident I was waiting in vain.

"Bring Toshiko Sekiya to me!" I finally shouted. The sound of my voice rang throughout the darkened theatre.

"She is not here," someone shouted back from offstage.

"Then get her here!" I roared. In spite of myself I lost my temper.

Miss Sekiya had gone blithely about her business. She was about to climb into her car and go home when my order was given to her. She came clattering back into the theatre and onstage in her high heels. For a long time I just stared at her.

Finally I said: "It appears that you don't have the slightest idea of how to act. First of all, why are you wearing high heels? I expressly told you not to wear any shoes. But you did. As a result, you come stumbling onstage clicking like a cricket and plunge us all into darkness by stupidly tripping over the lighting cable. What kind of angel is that?"

She meekly stood in front of me and stared.

"I can forgive what you did," I continued; "but when you know you have made a mistake, will you at least come and apologize? Just who do you think you are?"

All the time I sat scolding her I was slapping my knee in emphasis of what I said. The more I talked, the more I slapped my knee, and the more she stood trembling and speechless. Finally I waved her away. I got up and nearly pitched on my face. I had hit myself so hard my knee was bruised and swollen.

The earth traveled in its orbit about the sun forty times between the months I passed alone on the mountain overlooking the scenes of my childhood and the moment my steps on the path of Zen brought me to priesthood. For when I returned to Japan from Hollywood and once again took up the manner of living which is my heritage, my long experience and practice in Zen came to a head in the judgment of the Zen masters in Tokyo who had followed my progress over the years. My study and practice weighed sufficient to admit me to the supreme test of a Zen disciple.

I did not desire or ask to become a priest of Zen. I was chosen to become one. And I was examined for acceptance in the fashion that has been followed by those of Zen for centuries: by the *koan*.

One factor which contributed to my being selected to become a priest of Zen was my work on behalf of Zen in the United States. My forming the Zen study group in New York in 1927 was recalled favorably. That step had led to an alliance with Zen leaders in Japan. Sasaki, when he returned, had spoken well of my efforts.

The consistent pattern of my practice and study was a factor, too; for, as well as on my own, I had studied under the Zen masters in Tokyo while I was in Japan prior to going to Paris in 1937. Also, my play on the life of Buddha did much to express the understanding and realization I had of Zen, and my espousement of its way.

Accordingly, I was called before a court of six priests

and asked the certain *koans* which would determine the true degree and nature of my immersion in Zen. My responses revealed many things.

Satori is, as I have said, the measure of Zen. The *satori* experience is a sign, an indication that he who has experienced it has reached the very heart of Zen and felt the unfolding of the mind, the inner self or super-consciousness, in its fullness. *Satori* is the awakening of the mind to realization of *prajna*, that higher spiritual power—the highest form of human intuition—by which he who experiences *satori* comes in direct contact with reality itself instantaneously and takes a step toward oneness with the universe.

Any attempt I can make fully to explain the *satori* experience would be futile. For it does not belong in the category of relativity, as Suzuki has rightly pointed out in his writings, and, therefore, "it is not at all communicable in any ordinary logical way." *Satori* is nothing which may be imparted by a medium of communication such as language. As a Western mind expressed it, "It [*satori*] is a new view of life and of the universe which must be felt."

Just as *satori* is the measure of Zen, the *koan* is the measure of *satori*. The asking of koans enables the Zen masters, the priests, to test a disciple, for though he who experiences *satori* will have no doubt, the test by *koan* will affirm certainty absolutely.

The ultimate communication of Zen is through intuition, without words—speaking. The experienced Zen master can many times affirm the *satori* experience of a disciple intuitively. If not, then by asking *koans*.

The six priests who judged me for Zen priesthood sat cross-legged in a row like sentinels lined across a gate. I sat in similar fashion before them on a mat. I was dressed in a black kimono. *Tabi* (socks) clothed my feet. My head was bare.

The testing began.

"Before your father and mother, your great-grandfather and great-grandmother, thousands and thousands of years before they were born," the soft, wind-like voice of the high priest intoned, "who were you?"

My reply was in my attitude. No word was spoken by me. By concentration the priests' keen minds penetrated into mine, probed and fathomed my response.

There was silence for a time. Then the voice asked: "You have cut off two heads of the snake. If you cut off both heads of the snake, look at the sword against the clear sky. What do you feel, in that state of mind?"

Once again, silence. The minds of the priests became mirrors to my unspoken reply.

The questioning continued until, after a silence of what seemed hours, the high priest pronounced judgment: "You are worthy to be among us."

Had I not passed, the silence would have been shattered by the ring of the gong which sat beside the high priest. The ringing of it would have signaled failure and the end of the testing.

It is impossible for me to answer the *koans* I was asked here. There are traditional responses, which have been recorded, but there is no inflexible response to any one *koan*. Each one who undertakes the way of Zen must answer the *koans* for himself, else they are valueless, and he is deceived, and strives futilely, who gives superficial answers.

Being deemed worthy is not all there is to becoming a priest of Zen. Zen has its pomp and ritual too. There is an ordaining ceremony.

Some days after the test of the *koans* I joined twenty other priests before the altar of the temple and prayed to Buddha. I prostrated myself, my arms stretched out before me, my palms up, my forehead to the floor. Then, as I lay there I felt the encumbrance of my being drift away, my mind become nothing, yet everything. I felt the bare feet of Buddha standing upon my upturned palms, his essence penetrating throughout my consciousness. I became nothing: no Sessue Hayakawa, no actor, no wanderer in the world of men.

When I arose, on command, the crown-like silk hat of the priest was placed upon my head. Thus I reached another plateau of my journey. And as I left the temple later there echoed in my mind Buddha's summing up of his teaching:

> Cease to do evil;
> Learn to do well;
> Cleanse your own heart—
> This is the way of the Buddhas.

Destiny is indeed strange. To an extent, a man's destiny is predictable. That is to say that from a given cause an effect can be expected.

But in the ultimate, destiny is enigmatic. No one ever really can know absolutely what the end result of a certain turn of events will be, no matter what the beginning indications are.

For at what point in the eternal does the course of a man's fate begin? Who can say? Destiny takes hold we know not where, expands from the past through the present and into the future in an inevitable pattern as long as man is bound to the world of birth and death by karmic causation and is subject to the acumen of his deeds.

This way of thinking is a sort of fatalism, but I believe man's life-path does not consist of a mere accumulation of accidental events. For the most part it is predestined.

Kindred to predestination is the word "premonition."

In Japanese, premonition is *yokan*, a before-hand feeling. It is the sensing one has that he is going to win or lose, experience success or failure.

The events of my life have strung themselves on the thread of my existence like beads. Each happening has slid into place in order with a design basically not of my making. I have been merely allowed to make variations.

After I returned to Japan from war-enforced exile in Paris, I had cause to believe my career had entered upon a hiatus. I resumed life in the company of my family, entered into the priesthood of Zen and was active to a somewhat static extent in Japanese films. The greatest enrichment of my life in this phase was my embrace of Zen on that level on which one moves closer to nirvana. In that state one transcends the illusion of the world which persists when one clings to the dualism which relegates oneself to the slavery of the world of birth and death.

But I did not reckon, nor could I, not knowing, with the mind of an author and the impact of his book.

The author was Pierre Boulle. His book, first published in 1954, was *The Bridge over the River Kwai*.

12   The Bridge

THE NEW YORK *Times* CALLED IT: "ONE OF THE FRESHEST and most unusual tales to come out of World War II," *The Bridge over the River Kwai* (its title amended slightly for profound reasons involving the psychology of names) was fashioned into a motion picture beginning late in the autumn of 1956, in the jungle-laden mountains of Ceylon, where the entire film was shot.

Before the cameras began to roll in December, but for eight months prior to the shooting of the first scenes, several hundred native workers and forty-eight elephants labored to construct the railway bridge around which the plot and action of the story and film revolve. More than fifteen hundred trees were cut for the bridge. When the span was completed it measured one hundred yards in length. The railway tracks atop it were more than sixty feet above the surface of the river which swirled about its feet. The structure was a masterpiece. It cost $250,000, even with cheap labor.

While work on the bridge went on, Sam Speigel, the producer of the picture, contacted me in Japan. He telephoned from his suite in the Imperial Hotel in Tokyo and invited me to join the cast. "You're perfect for the part of Colonel Saito, the commandant of the Japanese prisoner of war camp," he said. "Just perfect. Can you meet with me here at the hotel?"

As far as I was concerned, this call came from a complete stranger. I frankly had no idea who Mr. Speigel was, and very little idea of what he had in mind.

"You'll be playing opposite Alec Guinness, if we can get him; and with William Holden. David Lean is directing," Mr. Speigel enthusiastically informed me.

I went to the Imperial Hotel and talked with him. After outlining the character of Colonel Saito, Mr. Speigel gave me a copy of the script to read and asked me to give him my answer as soon as I could. "The whole picture will be shot in Ceylon," he said. "The bridge is being built there now."

I told him I could say nothing until after I had read the script.

"Mr. Lean and most of the crew are in Ceylon getting set. I told him you are my choice for the role, but as a matter of courtesy I want his opinion. He hasn't seen anything of your recent work, so I took the liberty of sending him a print of *Tomoyuki Yamashita* to look at. The Toei company loaned it to me. I hope you don't mind."

"Not at all. What did Mr. Lean say?"

"I haven't heard from him yet. I'll let you know the moment that I do. In the meantime, Mr. Hayakawa, please read the script. It's a great one, and it's going to be a great film."

Playing the title role, I made *Tomoyuki Yamashita* early

in 1953. It is a film biography of the World War II military career of the infamous General Yamashita, the "Tiger of Malaya," whose activities during the war marked him for the death sentence he received following his trial for war crimes before the International Military Tribunal in Manila during the American Occupation. The film is a controversial one. Americans were approached to take roles in it, but refused because of the picture's anti-American leanings. Although there was little question of Yamashita's guilt, the film takes a sympathetic view of him. It whitewashes Yamashita by making it appear that responsibility for the atrocities committed under his command in the Philippines should really have been laid at the feet of Field Marshal Terauchi, an associate. Whatever the political implications of the film, and there were many, it provided me an opportunity to exercise fully my ability for characterization.

At home, when I skimmed through the script of *The Bride on the River Kwai* for the first time—quickly, looking for the high points and the scope of the role I had been asked to play, I immediately noted the absence of love interest, and that the entire story unfolded in the jungle. It did not excite me. I saw very little in it, in fact, and when Mr. Speigel telephoned a day or so later to ask my reaction, I told him I didn't think I would be interested.

"Please read it again," he urged me. "There's a tremendous story-impact there. Believe me."

I was dubious, but agreed to do so.

In the meantime, Tsuru read the script. She had one bit of advice to give me. "Do it," she said.

"But why?" I argued. "There's very little in it. No love interest. Nothing but two stubborn men, a Japanese and an Englishman, both army officers, clannish, duty-bound, proud, fighting within themselves and with each other in the middle of the sweltering jungle. And at the end of it all . . "

"Read the script again," she pleaded. "You do not sense what I sense."

"Perhaps not," I agreed. "Perhaps I have a preconception of what it should be, but isn't. I should keep an open mind."

"Go on, read it again," Tsuru urged. She put the script into my hand.

Inasmuch as Tsuru reads English somewhat better than I do there was considerable chance I was missing something. I went through the script again. I read it four times. Each time I did the story got better, more interesting. I began to visualize scenes and the drama of the conflict of wills, the clash of the East and West. I meditated, carefully weighing in my mind the question of whether I should do the part. I had to do so. I was unsure, skeptical.

I was not alone in my feeling. Halfway around the world from Tokyo, in England, Alec Guinness, whose performance was to win him an Academy Award, reacted the same way as I. The role of the Englishman, which he was asked to play, did not excite him. He said the role was one of "a dreary, unsympathetic man," and refused not once but three times. Even after reconsidering and finally accepting, he arrived in Ceylon with misgivings, brooded— according to newsmagazine reports, and after a few days on location in the jungle tried to quit.

But for a conclusion I finally drew, and which led to my telling Mr. Speigel I would play Saito, perhaps I would have turned down the role. As I read and reread the script, its power and message had come through.

War, the calamity of Mankind, reduced to its smallest and isolated definition, is not the rivalry of ideologies or the combat of great and strong nations; it is the battle of men and the minds of men.

And in the last extremity, the irreducible minimum, war is a man against a man: two human beings in opposition— sometimes fighting blindly on faith and orders with death-dealing weapons, at other times confronting one another with principles and strength of character, each seeking to advance his beliefs during a duel of wills. And such a duel of wills, "a contest of chivalries—*Bushido* v. What England Expects," *Time* called it when it reviewed the film, is the crux of *The Bridge on the River Kwai*. From the conflict of two men—Nicholson, the English colonel, and Saito, the Japanese colonel—stems all the power and the compelling emotional impact, the irony, anguish and pathos, the symbolization of the futility of war and the ridiculousness of what men fight for—the whole tragic human comedy encompassed by the film. With this image burning in my mind, I accepted the role of Colonel Saito.

"That's fine, fine," Mr. Speigel said when I told him he could count on me. "I'll make arrangements for you to join the others in Ceylon. By the way, I've heard from David Lean. He, too, wants you for Saito, but he says you're too fat. Wants you to lose at least fifty pounds."

"Too fat!" I roared with laughter. "I am a heavy, but not very heavy. Tell him not to worry."

My appearance in *Yamashita Hobun* had deceived David Lean into thinking I was built something like a *sumo-tori*, or professional Japanese wrestler, for whom three hundred pounds is not an uncommon weight.

It was a matter of fact that General Yamashita was such a mountain of a man. He weighed close to three hundred pounds, and when I portrayed him in the film I wore thick padding to make myself look as fat as he had been in life.

Technically a war picture, but one which expounds on the futility of war rather than on the glory obscenely attached to it by most war films, *The Bridge on the River Kwai* was made by some of the finest talent, under the worst of conditions. Work on the picture consumed fourteen months and $3,000,000. After agreeing to play the role of Colonel Saito and signing contracts, I left Japan in November, 1956, and, along with Alec Guinness, William Holden, Jack Hawkins, Geoffrey Horne and James Donald—each a principal member of the cast—passed five and a half months in Ceylon, on location, locked away from the rest of the world.

Never was a more diverse group of men ever gathered together. William Holden was all kindness, a good fellow. Guinness was polite, but aloof, much like myself. One got the idea he was present under duress. He was very much the typical Englishman. When he wasn't before the camera, he was off fishing—trying to lose himself in contemplation of some time and place many miles distant. There is something of the supernatural about him, I found. Indeed, like myself, he keenly believes in premonition. When he wasn't acting and transported by his art, or lost in reverie while fishing, he honestly loathed the conditions which made our lot one which smothered patience, frayed nerves and shortened tempers.

Every hour we spent in the jungle, in the abandoned stone quarry in which the prison camp of the film was established, was passed doing battle, within and without. For many—hundreds—in the cast and the technical crew, being on location was like being in prison. The tropical sun, a meridian sun, blazing with the intensity of a blast furnace, beat down without mercy. The humidity rarely measured below eighty-five per cent. When the hell-like heat of the sun wasn't tormenting us, the jungle was ripped by fierce electric storms. Driving rain, whipped wildly by harsh, biting winds sent us running for cover, sometimes five or six times a day. On some, the rain worked like the ancient Chinese water torture. Minds bent to match the chaos of the storms. The heat and humidity of the day and the night pushed more than one man to the end of his tether. Bickering became common, pettiness indigenous. The idleness of night and free time following work bred explosive unrest. Homesickness made men choleric and melancholy. The only relaxations were poker and 16-millimeter movies. And drink. Respite was at a premium.

At night we slept fitfully, naked, draped with towels to soak up the perspiration which incessantly beaded our bodies. We had electric fans, but they did little good. The air remained hot and disturbing just the same.

It was only once in a while that some beauty was found in the squalls which broke the unnerving silence of the night. Now and then thunder and lightning blasted out in a noisy pattern which gratified the senses. Dark clouds moved like specters in the deep blue night sky. Wind shook the jungle and made strange music. And when all abated and the moon came out there was momentary peace.

But it did not last. What nature gave she as quickly took away.

The jungle is a terrifying mistress. At length, its green beauty, starkly splashed with the blinding radiance of tropical flowers, does strange and awful things to men's minds. Congenial spirits are soon dulled. Although there was companionship in abundance, loneliness and desperation gripped many. Maddening, too, were the flies and other insects—strange and though small, indescribably irritating. They fed upon us, and thrived in countless numbers. "One day," Alec Guinness recalled when he was done with the film and back safe in England, "I killed 681 of them." This recollection is evidence enough of the neurotic nature that prevailed.

But for me this time of spiritual anguish and artistic accomplishment (two manifestations which have been coincident since man first attempted self-expression) was the time when the spirit of Zen permeated my whole being.

When the thunder rolled and the lightning flashed, I thought them beautiful. I moved secure in my sphere of discipline. Peace reigned in my soul.

My consistent display of calm intrigued those about me. They marveled at my control. Some questioned me. Some attempted to find something for themselves of what I possessed. But what I had nurtured for fifty years was not imparted in a few weeks. Still, to those who asked my help a measure of calm came.

In spite of the personal turmoil induced in just about all present on location, the work on the film progressed with rewarding results. The picture was not an easy one to make. Some of the work was dangerous. Death cast a shadow on one man, for instance, during one of the final scenes of the film, when the three commandos who come to destroy the bridge furtively make their way down the river to where it stands. They came down the river clinging to a raft on which were piled explosives and other detonating equipment. At one point on the journey the raft rocked through some rapids and the men were scattered in the wild water.

"Look out!" someone yelled.

All at once confusion reigned. There was a rush to the edge of the river where one of the men in charge of wardrobe unhesitatingly dived in to aid the three actors struggling in the swift water. Suddenly this young man disappeared, dragged down by the undercurrent. When he didn't come up, another man, a rope tied about his middle, plunged in after him. He brought him up gasping for air and clawing, momentarily out of his head. He lay on the ground threshing in a nervous fit until I secured him with a judo hold and the unit doctor was able to give him an injection. He was some hours regaining his senses.

In the meantime the others had been swept tumbling

downstream, where they hit a stretch of calm water and were able to save themselves.

On another occasion, however, a member of the crew was not so lucky. Nor would I have been, had not destiny intervened and kept me out of harm's way.

During the early phase of shooting the film we were quartered at a hotel in Columbo, the capital of Ceylon, from which we were driven daily to scene locations spotted at various places outside the city.·

"Your car will be leaving in a few minutes," one of Mr. Lean's assistants said to me one morning when I entered the hotel lobby after breakfast. "The driver will meet you in front."

I nodded my thanks and lighted a cigar. As the first smoke drifted toward the ceiling in a thick cloud a queer shiver enveloped me. My impulse was to let the car go without me. Although I was ready to go, and went out to meet it, at the last moment I grasped the excuse of having to go to the washroom. The car drove away without me.

On its way to the location the driver lost control, and the vehicle swerved off the road and into a tree. One of the occupants was killed. The dead man might well have been I, I reflected when news of the accident was brought. But for premonition I would have gone in the car as planned. But I sensed danger. Warning had flashed into my mind like inspiration. Why I cannot fully explain.

One of the things that characterized my first days on location in Ceylon was the deference with which I was treated. Almost everyone there looked upon me as an old man. They had heard about my career in silent films and that it had begun before the First World War, and concluded I should be indulged and treated like ancient china. Everyone, Guinness, Holden and David Lean especially, made it their job to take good care of me. I was impressed by the polite treatment I received, but piqued when I found out most of it was due to the conclusion I was old.

When the script called for me to do something strenuous, or when we had to walk through a rough bit of country, I was virtually shadowed—kept an eye on—by a crew member. I was always being given assistance. When we drove to a location no one would get into the car until I had done so and seated myself first. The same thing happened when we went to the mess hall for meals. Alec Guinness made it his habit, if he was ahead of me, to step aside so that I could enter first. This sort of treatment began to wear thin after a while. I became disgusted. So when I got into a playful wrestling match and won handily, I was glad. The concern for Hayakawa the old man ceased. The kindness and politeness, however, did not. Despite the trying conditions everyone was most cordial.

My relationship with David Lean was particularly good. Of necessity he is something of a solitary traveler in his profession. He has a keen mind. His insight is deeply penetrating. In his role of director he sees not only the fragments which, woven together, make the whole composition of a film, but the entirety as well. "He shows a rare sense of humor and a feeling for the poetry of situation," one critic wrote after seeing *The Bridge on the River Kwai*; "and he shows the even rarer ability to express these things, not in lines but in lives."

Mr. Lean and I enjoyed an excellent rapport when we worked together. We never found ourselves in opposition. But he was less than slightly beloved by some of his associates being broiled by the hot sun and infernal humidity of Ceylon during the stifling months we were isolated there. For one member of the technical crew was later quoted as having said, "Lean! That bloody perfectionist! He shot thirty seconds of film a day and then sat on a rock and stared at his goddam bridge!"

Perhaps he did appear to drag his heels. But he achieved all he desired to achieve. He explored the subject of his responsibility carefully, and was most solicitous when it came to dealing with us, the actors. I never witnessed an instance of his abusing any actor, although it was later revealed that he all but alienated Alec Guinness; for, when Mr. Guinness reported to Ceylon from London, Mr. Lean offhandedly informed him that he had really wanted Charles Laughton for the role of Colonel Nicholson. It was some days before Mr. Guinness' unhappiness over this abated. Until it did, the coolness with which each man regarded the other was almost solid enough to be seen.

As a director, David Lean is one who is acutely aware of the psychology of the actor, of all that motivates theatrical presence as distinct from private. He never discourages. He always makes every effort to assist and to bring out the best in one.

The tone and quality of the various scenes Alec Guinness and I played in together in the film grew out of conferences we had with Mr. Lean. We three frequently got together and talked over the situations we were charged with creating. All of us had views and held them. We all made suggestions and combined our particular personal insights toward achieving what the circumstances demanded. But for Mr. Guinness, I think, the expression of his role was a matter of technique. He is not in real life as he appears to be on the screen. But though he may rely upon technique a great deal, his religious affinity with his profession is of a depth which precludes purely conscious motivation. He is not a natural actor. His artistry is the result of years of hard, diligent work.

But for me, technique is impossible. At the root of my acting and, in this instance, at the root of my portrait of Colonel Saito, is Zen. Zen, which, in its intuitive grasp of final reality, achieves the elimination of the unnecessary. Zen strips off all the artificial wrappings humanity devises. The result is a oneness. Such oneness I had with Colonel Saito.

All of us know that physical appearance can be deceiving. It is not an inflexible index to the character and nature of a person. But in films and on the stage physical appearance is used as the first definition. Types, based greatly on preconceptions, are important. Hollywood, for instance, long ago established certain stock characters. In some cases, type of character literally has been parceled out by nationality.

Since the very first time a Japanese military officer was represented in an American motion picture, a type persistently has been portrayed. Japanese officers in Hollywood films invariably are personifications of evil. They are little brown-skinned men whose almond eyes shine with cunning, and whose mouths twist into cruel and revolting shapes as they hiss inhumane commands, threaten torture with sadistic indifference through protruding teeth. They are caricatures rather than characters.

I am proud to say I have never played such roles. I have portrayed Japanese officers, but mine have been men. The untrue stereotype I find distasteful—not because it insults the Japanese so much, but because it is not true to life. It is not human. But, until recent years, Hollywood insisted upon making Japan a nation of insensitive evil-doers devoid of compassion—heartless and wantonly cruel.

Thanks to my friend Erich Von Stroheim the same view was taken of Germans. Once he strode upon the screen in *Hearts of the World* the die was cast until he, himself, broke the mold with his portrayals in *La Grand Illusion* and *Five Graves to Cairo*. Then, and only then, was it brought out that German officers had souls. It was left for me to bring the dimension of humanity to the Japanese military officer. I had a beginning in *Three Came Home.* The full flower of success came with Colonel Saito.

I did not think of the Colonel as a sympathetic character, but to me he was a decent sort of man, one tightly hemmed in by the demands of his profession, his obligation to duty. His destiny was to battle within himself and lose. It was my destiny to portray him, and by my portrait to open my future to greater vistas. Saito and I became indivisible. The Zen state of *muga* made us one and the same.

When I stepped before David Lean's camera, Sessue Hayakawa disappeared and Saito presented himself. It was he who stood before the ragged, bone-weary British soldiers, dispatched from Singapore to do his bidding, and who said: "I hate the British. You're here, under my personal command, to carry out a job which is necessary for the victory of the Japanese Grand Army. I want to tell you, once and for all, that I won't have my orders questioned in any way. I hate the British. Noncompliance will be punished severely. Discipline must be maintained. If any of you are thinking of putting up a show of resistance, let me remind you that I've got power of life and death over the lot of you. I shan't think twice about exercising that power. . . . The death of the whole lot of you is a mere trifle to a senior officer of the Japanese Grand Army."

These words began my first speech in *The Bridge on the River Kwai.* At Mr. Lean's suggestion I spoke it at one sweep. It lasted nine minutes, ending when I keynoted the conflict to come, saying: "Work will begin at dawn tomorrow. You will parade here on the first blast of the whistle. The officers will fall in as well. They'll form a separate squad of their own, and they'll be expected to get through the same amount of work as the rest of you. Tools will be issued, and the Japanese engineer will give you his instructions. That's all I have to say this evening. But I'd like to remind you of General Yamashita's motto: 'Be happy in your work.' Just bear that in mind."

Colonel Saito! In all the films I have made, no character captivated or challenged me more. He came to grip me, to control me.

As the two colonels, Alec Guinness and I played a scene in which the Japanese tries to sway the Englishman to negate his demand that officers will not work. Saito's demand that they do is the seed of the conflict between Nicholson and himself. Nicholson justifies his position that officers must not work like ditchdiggers, by quoting international law and the tenets of the Hague Convention. Saito ignores the argument. He remains adamant in his position as a despot consecrated to duty. Nicholson refuses to yield, even to the threat of death, and his men support him.

In an effort to sway Nicholson, Saito chooses to try kindness where force has failed. He has the British colonel to supper and plies him with good food, cigars and whisky. But Nicholson will not budge.

Saito's response is immediate, hysterical anger. He becomes beside himself with fury.

At that point, I found myself roaring, bawling—screaming in tantrum. Unperturbed, Guinness looked at me, arose from the table, turned and started for the door. There was nothing more to be said. The scene was ending.

But as he moved to leave I heard myself yelling, "Stop there! Stay where you are! Don't move! Guards!"

The lines were not in the script. They came instantaneously to my mind, spontaneously out of my mouth, on the provocation of situation, as Saito would act and react, for I myself would have remained silent and curbed my emotion.

"What would you write to your wife in a case like this?" David Lean asked me shortly before we shot the scene where Saito, crushed and brought to his knees by the wisdom of the West, prepares to rescue the last of his honor through disemboweling himself. "You are going to commit suicide tomorrow," he sketched. "What would you write?"

Rice paper, a brush and Japanese ink were brought to me. I thought over what Saito would say, what I would say, as the son of the samurai.

Writing the letter took time. Every stroke of the brush was emotion. The letter was to be Saito's final word to his wife and children. I wrote of failure, broken dreams and lost hope, of honor in death; and into the letter I put my very being.

As I wrote, Mr. Lean observed and remarked, "I've never seen a man concentrate so in writing."

Indeed, I was lost in thought and memory; and for a moment which was timeless—for time had stopped—all that I had come to then became all that I was. I had come full cycle. In my mind's eye I saw myself at eighteen in Nanaura writing my own letter of farewell. What had been and what was came together for an instant. Locked in concentration, I saw eternity loom gateless before me. Destiny once again gave me a sign.

Completed late in 1957, *The Bridge on the River Kwai* was successively premiered in New York, Paris, Hollywood, London and Tokyo. I was asked to be present at the New York and Hollywood openings. I was in Tokyo at the time, and flew from there to New York and, after the premiere at the Palace Theatre in Times Square on December 18, 1957, back to Hollywood.

The acclaim the film received following the New York opening was tremendous. The critics raved about everything. "In the line of performance," Bosley Crowther applauded in the *New York Times* the next morning, "Alec Guinness does a memorable—indeed, classic—job in making the ramrod British colonel a profoundly ambiguous type. With a rigid, serene disposition, he displays the courage and tenacity of a lion, as well as the denseness and pomposity of a dangerously stupid, inbred snob. He shows beneath the surface of a hero, the aspects of an inhuman fool . . ."

Then he got to me: "As his Japanese opposite number, old Sessue Hayakawa is superb—brutal, stubborn, sluggish—an equally grotesque fool."

Jammed with superlatives, the *Times* review was spread across four columns. It heralded what was to come: Eight Motion Picture Academy of Arts and Sciences Oscar nominations, distribution and acclaim in forty-five countries, financial success totaling more than $26,000,000.

Yet Guinness had bemoaned the "dreary, unsympathetic" Colonel Nicholson; and I had not at first seen the power of the story, the potential of the conflict of wills.

But destiny brought us together.

For my performance as Colonel Saito, I was nominated to receive the Academy Award for "Best Supporting Actor." But I did not win it. Guinness won top honors for best actor. David Lean was given an Oscar for best direction. But Hayakawa did not win. Instead, I was presented the Golden Globe Award of the Hollywood Foreign Press Association. This sign of success was enough and at the same time unnecessary. I never think of failure or success. When I finish a motion picture or a play, it is not my endeavor, not my achievement. It is the hand of destiny.

It is the hand of destiny, too, which has brought me renewed acclaim since *The Bridge on the River Kwai*. No sooner did I return to Tokyo from New York and Hollywood than I was entreated to return and appear on television, in more motion pictures—*Green Mansions*, for one—and on Broadway in *Kataki*, a play of two characters, an American and a Japanese—soldiers, marooned on an island in the Pacific.

Destiny has brought me much. She has been kind. But it has been left to me to fashion the acumen of deeds in the pattern destiny has drawn, to solve the great *koan* of life for myself.

More than seven centuries ago, as man measures time, the Zen master Mumon wrote timeless words:

> The great path has no gates,
> Thousands of roads enter it.
> When one passes through this gateless gate
> He walks freely between heaven and earth.

I am one traveling toward the gateless gate. I have come far. And along the way, I have stopped and caught a glimpse of the future where waits entry into the infinity of the eternal and inexplicable. There I will be beyond the world of birth and death. Time then will stop. I will be as one with the universe.

The path has wound upward from the depths and darkness of despair to the fulfillment of bright being. Thus far, as it has in the past, as it will in the future, Zen has shown me the way.

"How shall I escape from the Wheel of Birth and Death?" *a disciple one day whined to his master. Came the reply: "Who puts you under restraint?"*

THE END